NO
BOUNDARIES

NO BOUNDARIES

Passion and Pain On and Off the Pitch

Ronnie Irani

with Richard Coomber

JOHN BLAKE

Published by John Blake Publishing Ltd,
3 Bramber Court, 2 Bramber Road,
London W14 9PB, England

www.johnblakepublishing.co.uk

First published in hardback in 2009

ISBN: 978-1-84454-861-3

British Library Cataloguing-in-Publication Data:

A catalogue record for this book is available from the British Library.

Design by www.envydesign.co.uk

Printed in the UK by CPI William Clowes Beccles NR34 7TL

1 3 5 7 9 10 8 6 4 2

Papers used by John Blake Publishing are natural, recyclable products made
from wood grown in sustainable forests. The manufacturing processes
conform to the environmental regulations of the country of origin.

I would like to take this opportunity to thank my wife Lorraine for just allowing me to be Ronnie Irani! Looking forward to life after professional cricket with her and my two daughters Simone and Maria. I love you guys so much. My mum and dad Anne and Jimmy for being tough but fair while I was growing up. You have always been there for me whatever my situation. The mother-in-law Pat who I hope enjoys life in the west wing; put the kettle on chuck!

If you are not living life on the edge you are taking up to much room!

CONTENTS

CHAPTER 1   'HE'S BIG AND HE'S BARMY'   1

CHAPTER 2   NUTS ABOUT BRAZIL   5

CHAPTER 3   THE VIEW FROM MY BEDROOM WINDOW   17

CHAPTER 4   STOP ME IF YOU'RE FEELING FRUITY   31

CHAPTER 5   CHIRPING GOD   41

CHAPTER 6   MY PAL, THE WANNABE PORN STAR   55

CHAPTER 7   SOMEWHERE NEAR THE DARTFORD   65
             TUNNEL

CHAPTER 8   LOSTOCK TO CHELMSFORD – THE   75
             LONGEST JOURNEY

CHAPTER 9   ARE YOU WATCHING, LANCASHIRE?   81

CHAPTER 10   A YOUNG THRUSTER   91

CHAPTER 11   WELL DONE, YOU'RE DROPPED   101

CHAPTER 12   THERE'S SHIT ON THE END OF YOUR BAT   111

CHAPTER 13   WE'RE THINKING OF SENDING YOU HOME   127

CHAPTER 14   I WANT TO BE A MOUNTAIN PERSON   137

CHAPTER 15   COCKSCOMB INJECTIONS   145

CHAPTER 16   ON YOUR BIKE   151

CHAPTER 17 YOU SHOULD INVEST IN DOT.COM 163

CHAPTER 18 LEAVE ENOUGH GAP TO CREATE A SPARK 175

CHAPTER 19 YOU'RE THE MAN TO TAKE SACHIN 183

CHAPTER 20 A LONG STRETCH IN SYDNEY 193

CHAPTER 21 AT TIMES IT'S LIKE BEING A SINGLE MUM 207

CHAPTER 22 THE GAME THAT NEVER WAS 215

CHAPTER 23 POOFS AND PIRATES 229

CHAPTER 24 MIND GAMES TO WIN GAMES 241

CHAPTER 25 I'LL BE FRANC, IT'S FRIGHTENING 257

CHAPTER 26 WHAT'S IT ALL ABOUT, ALFI? 265

CHAPTER 1
'HE'S BIG AND HE'S BARMY'

There was a lump in my throat even before I opened the door to make the familiar walk down the steps of Chelmsford pavilion. It was a packed house for a Twenty20 match under floodlights and, as usual, I was wearing the Essex shirt with the red, blue and yellow badge. But I wasn't playing. I would never play again. I knew it and so did the fans. As I reached the pitch they got to their feet and started to sing:

'His name is Ronnie Irani
'He's big and he's barmy
'He bats number five for Essex
'ESSEX!
'All the kids in the street shout
'Hey big lad, what's your name?
'His name is Ronnie Irani...'

I blinked away the tears, took a firm hold of Simone and Maria's hands and started the most memorable walk of my life.

1

A million thoughts tumbled through my head as I slowly circled the ground with my young daughters, also in their Essex shirts with their names on the back. I could only wave and soak up the emotion of the night. There was no way of telling the fans how much they meant to me. They had adopted a big, raggy-arsed kid from Bolton as one of their own after his dream of playing for Lancashire turned sour. I'd got to know some of them well – Malcolm Singer and his mates, Ian, Anthony and Peter; Tony and Pam and their three daughters; and the late 'Del Boy' whose spirit was always with me whenever I walked down those steps and who I hope is 'forever blowing bubbles'. Hundreds of others had become familiar faces over the years.

There had been better cricketers at the club, yet somehow the Essex fans picked me out for special attention. I like to think it was because I put all I had into every single ball, whether bowling, batting or chasing around the boundary, and also because, while I played the game hard and to win, I never lost sight of the fact that it was meant to be fun for me and entertaining for them. Some players avoid the fans if they can, but I thoroughly enjoyed the craic and exchanging banter with them. And I believe both the Essex fans and England's 'Barmy Army' found it possible to identify with me. They couldn't imagine themselves being Brian Lara or Graeme Hick or Wasim Akram, but they could look at me and think that, if things had been a bit different, they might have been that big bugger whose enthusiasm, hard work and desire to succeed had made the most of his natural talent.

The people of Essex backed me from the day I stepped off the train in Chelmsford, with everything I owned packed into four bags and with only nine first-class matches to show for my five years at Lancashire. Even when England selectors and officials decided I wasn't good enough or was too much of 'a character' to be bothered with, the people of Essex were still on my side. Above all, they had enjoyed the great times for club and country that had made the last 19 years so unforgettable.

I looked up at the box I'd hired for the night. I'd wanted to share the moment with as many of the most important people in my life as I could, including my wife Lorraine, who I'd been with since she was 16, Mum and Dad who had instilled in me their work ethic and love of cricket and who had followed every step of my career, my secretary Linda Bennett, business partners Nick Bones and Aimee and Damian Donzis, Charles Lord from Stuart Surridge who had sponsored me, Rowland Luff the best man at my wedding, and my mentor John Bird. There were many more who I wished could have been there, people who had given me a leg up when I needed it most.

I went over and gave George Clarke a hug. George was the Essex dressing-room attendant and had not only been the first person to welcome me to Chelmsford all those years before but had also been a brave enough umpire to give England legend Graham Gooch out lbw when I bowled to him in my first Essex practice match. That had been an early feather in my cap and helped establish me at my new home. I spotted Graham Saville on the committee-room balcony and waved to him. I trusted him so much that I'd quit Lancashire just on his word that Essex would sign me and, together with Goochie and Keith Fletcher, Sav had guided me through my career from rookie to county captain.

Ironically, I had been at the peak of my form when Richard Steadman, the top knee specialist in the world, told me, 'I'm sorry, Ronnie. It's time to call it a day.' It hurt like hell but I knew that, if he said nothing more could be done to patch up a knee that had troubled me since I was 17 years old, then that was it. I'd been on a rollercoaster of emotions since breaking the news, first to Lorraine and then to the management and my team-mates at Essex. I was easily moved to tears, especially when I read the tribute Graham Gooch paid me in the press: 'His attitude and work ethic have always been spot-on since he joined us 13 years ago. He has never lost his appetite and self-belief and, in his book, there was never such a thing as a lost cause. That was something that lifted everyone around him. At both one-day level as well as in the championship he led by example and produced many match-winning performances that confirmed his status as a superb player.'

It just doesn't get any better than to have one of the greatest players, top leaders and an outstanding man say things like that about you.

It had been a fabulous career – I'd scored lots of runs, taken my share of wickets, picked up trophies, set a record for my country, made some lasting friends, had some great laughs and travelled the world. But I have to say that the greatest single moment was feeling the love from the fans at Chelmsford that night as I walked round the ground with my two 'Essex girls'.

As I completed my lap of honour, I saw a familiar face in the crowd. 'Kush' Dave and his son had been among the first supporters to get behind me. It was he who had started my special song. I went over to him, gave him my last Essex shirt and said, 'Thanks, pal. It's been a ball.'

CHAPTER 2
NUTS ABOUT BRAZIL

It only took a couple of days for the harsh reality to become all too clear: I was 36 years old and out of work. At an age when most men are settled into a career and in many cases looking to move into a senior position, I was starting afresh, as though I'd just left school. When I looked at my CV, it was obvious that, as impressive as it might be to wield a lump of willow effectively from the age of six, or make a small, hard ball swing out or in at will, neither talent was much use for anything other than being a professional cricketer. There was an additional snag – in honing those skills, I had somewhat neglected my formal education. There was no degree to impress a would-be employer, indeed not so much as an A level.

I had some ideas I wanted to pursue. I already had my own insole company with partners in Germany and the USA and I had high hopes for that. But it was very much at the development stage and was costing me money rather than bringing it in. I needed something that would make the most of my other talents and, when I analysed what those were, it came down to a willingness to work hard, boundless enthusiasm, a sense of humour and an ability to talk – some would say an inability to shut up.

Thanks to my natural gift of the gab, I was already commanding quite good money on the after-dinner-speaking circuit, and I would now have time to do more of that. And as Essex captain, I'd done a fair amount of broadcasting, which came quite easily to me, so at the back of my mind I thought I could probably follow some of my fellow ex-professionals into the media.

I'd been standing on my hind legs and speaking for about as long as I could remember. In my early days as a teenager at Lancashire, I would be asked to go along to a local cricket club or school and present prizes, sometimes to kids not much younger than I was. And usually someone would ask, 'Would you mind saying a few words?' I did mind, a lot. It was embarrassing. I'd mutter something about congratulations on last season and good luck for next season then try to get off as quickly as possible. I could chat forever in the dressing room, much to the annoyance of some of my senior colleagues who felt I should remember my place and shut up, but this was different. This was performing solo and I only felt comfortable doing that out in the middle of a cricket pitch. I felt like a plonker every time I had to speak and was tempted to turn down these invitations but then I remembered how good I'd felt when England footballer Francis Lee came to my cricket club at Heaton, and the excitement around the place when Olympic sprinter Allan Wells visited our school and showed us his gold medal. I reasoned that, if these people could put themselves out for a nobody from Bolton like me, the least I could do was to get over my nervousness and talk to a few kids from time to time.

Over the years, it became second nature to speak in front of people for a couple of minutes, but that was a lot different from my first proper 'gig' as an after-dinner speaker. By the time Woodford Wells Cricket Club invited me to speak at their presentation night, I was an England player and beginning to be a favourite among the Essex supporters.

'Just come along and hand out the prizes and maybe talk for about 20 minutes,' the secretary suggested, smiling encouragingly.

I didn't like to tell him I'd never done anything like that before. I swallowed hard, agreed and then thought, What the hell do I talk about?

The shadow of that speech hung over me for several days. To say I was panicking would be an exaggeration, but not much of one. I started to scribble down all the questions fans usually asked me. Who's the fastest bowler you've batted against? What's it like facing a bouncer that flies at your head? Who was your favourite player when you were growing up? Who was the better captain – Mike Atherton or Graham Gooch? Who is the funniest guy in the Essex dressing room? What does it feel like to drop a catch? I reckoned, if I strung the answers to those into a series of stories, I would probably be OK, although I wasn't sure if cricket was going to be high on the agenda when my formal invitation arrived and I saw that the other speaker was a guy called Sid Dennis, a scrap-metal merchant from Skegness. Wonder why they want to hear about the scrap-metal business? I thought.

As it happened, I turned up at the venue at the same time as Sid and the fact that he was driving an E-class Mercedes suggested there must be plenty of money in being a 'metal-materials recycler', as he described his job on the card he handed me. Sid looked like a dodgy nightclub bouncer. He weighed 20-odd stones, his head was as smooth as a polished egg, and, if owners grow to resemble their dogs, Sid definitely had a bulldog or two back in Skegness.

I sat next to him on the top table, looking out at a sea of around 300 faces. I was shitting myself. My nerves weren't improved when one of the club members came up to ask for an autograph and said, 'I'm really looking forward to your speech.' Suddenly I realised that *I* was the entertainment and these people's enjoyment of the evening was at least in part down to me. I confessed to Sid that I was an after-dinner virgin and feeling as nervous as hell.

He smiled reassuringly. 'Don't worry, lad, you're not dead yet. You'll be reet here. Every speaker is only as good as the crowd and this lot are OK. Just remember, they want to know what it's like to be a professional cricketer. They would love to be able to do what you do, to meet the people you meet, and to be in that dressing room, padded up and waiting to go out to bat in front of thousands of people. Talk about what you know and they'll love it.'

Just before I stood up, Sid slipped me a piece of paper and said, 'Kick off with that.'

I read what he'd written, memorised it and got to my feet, gripping my notes firmly and hoping people couldn't see how much they were shaking. 'Good evening,' I said, my mouth as dry as an Indian wicket. 'For those of you who don't know me, my name is Ronnie Irani and I play cricket for Essex. I should tell you that I wasn't born in Essex but, one thing's for sure, I could fucking die here tonight.'

The audience roared with laughter. The ice was broken and I started to feel a bit better. Thanks, Sid.

I went through my stories and the audience seemed to be

interested and even laughed in the right places. By the time I reached my final story, I was enjoying myself.

I said, 'You are probably wondering what it's like in the dressing room before a big match. It varies a lot according to the captain. Graham Gooch is quietly encouraging, while others try to gee you up with a rousing speech, like Mike Atherton before the Test at Edgbaston. Ath was obviously feeling Churchillian. He stood before us and proclaimed, "What we have to ask ourselves is, are we men or are we boys? We are about to represent our country so it's time to decide if we are men or boys. The fans expect us to deliver a victory. Are we men or are we boys? Millions will be watching us around the world on TV. Are we men or are we boys?" At that moment the umpire knocked on the door and Mike yelled, "Come on, let's go, boys!"'

When I thought back, I wasn't sure it was Mike Atherton who'd said it – his final gee-up was usually: 'Let's fucking get out there' – but it was a good story and the audience laughed loudly then applauded as I sat down. One or two even stood up and clapped.

Sid squeezed my knee and said, 'Well done, lad. You did great.' Then he eased his way to his feet, looked out at the crowd and said, 'I'd like to thank Ronnie for his speech. I thought it was brilliant. Mind you, gentlemen, I've played a bit of cricket in my time and I don't fucking bang on about it like he does!' That got the biggest laugh of the night.

As we made our way to the cars afterwards, I thanked Sid and said, 'That's a great motor. It's even better than Graham Gooch's and he was captain of England. It must be worth at least fifty grand.'

'Fifty-five, lad, and paid for by doing stuff like this. You did well tonight. You can do this. You need to sharpen up a bit but that will come with experience. I'll see you around.'

Over the years, I've worked with a lot of fine comedians, people like Mike Farrell, Adger Brown, Jed Stone and Ian Richards, who can be guaranteed to put on a good show at any dinner. But Sid Dennis remains my favourite, partly because he's hilarious but mainly because of his generosity that night.

As I'll relate later, not all my gigs have gone as well as that one, but I managed to build up a decent reputation as a speaker who was not only entertaining but could also be relied on to turn up and not drop organisers in the shit at the last minute. However, as lucrative as the circuit can be, it wasn't going to be enough to pay all the bills and provide the funds to get the company up and running. I needed something else.

As well as cricket interviews on Sky, the BBC and Channel 4, I'd appeared on a number of TV shows as varied as *A Question of Sport*, kids' Saturday-morning programmes and the groundbreaking *TFI Friday* with Chris Evans and Will Macdonald, which was the only show where it seemed compulsory to down several pints before going on air. I've had a few nights on the lash with Chris and Will, including one where Chris tried to match Alan Brazil drink for drink and only realised he'd failed when he fell down the stairs while Alan strolled down nonchalantly. Chris is a terrific guy and for me one of the best broadcasters this country has produced in recent years. His radio work inspired me to get into it. Will is a brilliant producer and a keen cricket enthusiast like Chris, and is someone you can always rely on. A good mate.

Radio is my favourite medium. It is much more relaxed and spontaneous, more intimate. There's not the clutter of cameras and lights that inevitably make TV more formal. There's nothing between you and the listener but the microphone which allows you to chat to them in their homes, in their cars or on the beach. I'd always made myself available for interviews as a player and was happy for 5 live or talkSPORT to ring me up for a quick word and never dreamed of asking for payment. My first solo broadcast came when Kevin and Vicky Stewart, the owners of the Chelmsford-based station Dream FM, invited me to present the drive-time show every Friday night during the winter on the recommendation of my car sponsor Mike Lumsden of Mercedes Benz Direct. They really took a punt on my popularity as Essex captain and gave me loads of good advice, not least just to be myself and talk to the audience as though I was talking to a couple of people in a bar. I played some of my favourite music, chatted about sport and conducted my first interviews, many of them with mates like Jamie Redknapp, Jamie Theakston and Graham Gooch. Phil Tufnell even came into the studio for a chat and a laugh. It all seemed to go well and planted the seed that it might be something I could try when cricket was over.

Although cricket was my chosen profession, I'd had a passion for all sports since I was a kid. I grew up in a house in Bolton where the talk rarely moved off Manchester United in the winter and local cricket in the summer, with plenty to discuss about athletics, tennis, rugby league, horse racing or anything else that happened to be on the television in between. I even had a couple of snooker lessons with local legend Tony Knowles. So, while it may sound corny for me to say this in view of my present employment, talkSPORT really was my favourite radio station. I used to have it on in the car as I drove to and from training or matches and loved its mix of informed comment, banter and irreverence. They realised I was always happy to go into their studios and I was interviewed on the afternoon show by Paul Hawksbee and Andy Jacobs, and on Rhodri Williams's Sunday show. After one visit, Andy Townsend said, 'You want to keep in here. You never know – when you've finished playing, it might be something you could do.'

I must have done something right because, when Paul Hawksbee went on holiday one year, I was invited to sit in with Andy Jacobs. I said yes straight away and hastily rearranged my other commitments to leave my afternoons free. After a couple of training days with Matt Smith and a chat with Andy, I found myself on air as a co-host on one of the most popular shows in speech radio. Looking back, I know I wasn't that good but it was great experience and Andy was terrific, jumping in to rescue me whenever I started to struggle. My admiration for professional broadcasters went up enormously. It had never occurred to me that something as apparently simple as reading out an email or just holding a conversation with someone across the desk could be quite tricky in practice. You had to make it sound like you were chatting normally but without all the cutting across each other and half-finished sentences that you get among friends in a pub. Suddenly I realised that making it sound natural was harder than I'd thought.

For all the awkwardness I felt at times, I still enjoyed doing the show and the management clearly thought I had some potential because they asked if I would continue to do regular sessions. I was tempted but had to turn them down because it would have interfered with my cricket. But I kept in touch and, by great good fortune, when I was forced to hang up my cap, a vacancy came up to work as a pundit on their cricket coverage. Shortly after that, they offered me a regular spot alongside Alan Brazil on the breakfast show. It meant getting up at 3.30am, six days a week but I didn't think twice.

Working with Alan turned out to be a fabulous experience. He knows what it's like to make the transition from sport to radio and he helped me avoid many of the traps that lurk around the corner in live broadcasting. I was his first 'rookie' co-host but he was patient, generous and incredibly supportive.

Al may come across as a feisty Scot who just talks off the top of his head but everything he says is based on a profound knowledge and love of all sport and his exceptional ability as a communicator. There's hardly any subject that he isn't well informed about. I smile every time he comes out with 'As you realise, I know nothing about cricket' because I know he's just about to utter a gem that cuts right to the heart of whatever we are discussing.

To say that Al likes a drink is like saying Ian Botham relished beating the Australians. He once said to me, 'Ronnie, remember the glass is always half full,' but I don't think he could possibly know that because I've never seen him drink a half. There have been mornings, and remember I get to the studio along with the milkman at about a quarter to five – Al comes in about five to … well, let's leave it at five to – when I could swear he has come straight from whichever bar he was regaling with his stories. Yet he is still switched on to the latest news and ready to ask all the right questions of the guests. Once that studio light goes on to indicate we are live, he is the consummate professional. He was a hell of a striker in his day, especially in his time at Ipswich, but I would venture to suggest that he is an even better broadcaster.

He has a wicked sense of humour and loves to take the

mickey out of me. It was Al who gave me the nickname Vernon because he said I sound like Vernon Kay, who was also born in Bolton. He never misses the chance to tease me about my busted relationship with Nasser Hussain, or try to put me on the spot about some other member of the cricket fraternity that he knows I've fallen out with just as I'm bending over backwards to be fair to them.

Mind you, I'm not the only one who has to field his spiky probes. I remember England manager Duncan Fletcher coming into the studio to plug his autobiography and, after the usual pleasantries and some questions about the book, Alan said, 'Duncan, something I've always wanted to ask you. Why didn't you pick Ronnie more often?'

To his credit, Duncan didn't blink and assured Al that I had been close on a lot of occasions. Close but no cigar.

One of my favourite moments with Alan came during the sparring that goes on between him and Mike Parry just before the handover at ten o'clock. All through our programme that day we'd been playing snatches of our favourite music from films and Alan had been threatening the audience with what he claimed was my number-one choice, which he wouldn't even reveal to me. Mike Parry said that one of the main items on his show was to be whether or not funerals should be more cheerful, a celebration of the dead person's life rather than mourning for their passing. Al cut across him and said, 'Mike, got to interrupt because we have to play Ronnie's favourite film track. I think it's perfect for a happy funeral,' and as he faded up the sound I heard the kids from *The Sound of Music* sing: 'So long, farewell, auf wiedersehen, goodbye.'

Brilliant! And typical of the man who has helped make my transition from cricketer to broadcaster such a positive experience. Sometimes, when I look across the desk at him at six in the morning, it's hard to realise he is the same person I used to watch run out for Manchester United when I was just 15 years old. It's at moments like that I reflect on what an incredible journey I've enjoyed.

CHAPTER 3

THE VIEW FROM MY BEDROOM WINDOW

If ever a kid was destined to become a cricketer it was me. From 26 October 1971, when I weighed in at 8lb 6oz, I was surrounded by the sights, sounds and smells of the game. Mum and Dad took me home to our house in the mining town of Atherton in Lancashire but, by the time I really became aware of what was going on around me, they had bought a house in Bolton, on the boundary at Heaton Cricket Club. From then until I left home in 1994, I slept in a bedroom with a window overlooking the pitch and, as a child, the outfield became my playground.

My dad, Jimmy Irani, came to England from his home in Bombay, where his grandfather had settled to avoid persecution in his native land, then known as Persia. Dad claims that, when he arrived here in 1961 to play cricket, he only intended to stay six months but he got captured by a pretty 16-year-old Lancashire lass named Anne Main and has been here ever since.

I guess my great-grandfather was the first in our line to be called Irani, which means of Iran. I don't know if it was a slur in 19th-century India but there have often been comments about it since, especially in the last few years as the political scene in that part of the world has made the headlines. I think Dad suffered some abuse when he first came to England in what was a much more racist time than now, but he was helped by the fact that even then cricket was a multi-racial sport, so he was soon accepted because he was a good player and no one noticed his name any more.

It never really bothered me, though there was an incident when I was about eight involving my first playground girlfriend that sticks in my mind. She was cute and we used to play in the same group and I seem to remember I once snatched a tentative kiss. But one morning she came up to me and said, 'I told my mum my boyfriend was Ronnie Irani and she said, "Why are you going out with a Paki?"' It was the first time I'd realised my name was unusual for a lad from Bolton and suddenly all the other kids were teasing me. I was hurt and confused. It only lasted a few days but, at an age when you desperately want to fit in, it was embarrassing and was definitely part of my toughening-up process.

I never had the chance to get to know Dad's family. His mother died young, shortly after he arrived in England, which I know knocked him back because, in those days when plane travel was out of reach of ordinary people, he wasn't able to get home to see her before she passed or to attend the funeral. He talked to me about her, about how strong she was, and I wish I'd met her. His father visited us in England. I don't remember him, although there is a picture of him holding me as a baby and I still have a gold rattle that he gave me with 'Prince Ronnie' engraved on it. I knew Mum's family well – her mother and grandmother were still alive when I was young and there were my aunties Janet and Glad and uncles Johnny, Phil and Ian. It was a tight-knit family and into sport in a big way.

To say Dad loves his cricket is a bit like saying Alex Ferguson likes to win football matches. He played every year until a heart-valve operation forced him to quit in 1999, aged 64. He was captain of Daisy Hill Cricket Club for 12 years and every Saturday and Sunday our family would go to matches, Dad playing, Mum helping with the teas and me just soaking it all up like a sponge. Most of my early memories are of running around the outfield during breaks in play, messing around on the swings and slides or being in pavilions, surrounded by men dressed in white. As soon as I was big enough, I would prepare Dad's cricket bag, whiten his boots and rub linseed oil into his bat. It was a labour of love – and also earned me 50p.

I had a toy bat almost as soon as I could walk and Dad would 'bowl' a spongy ball to me in the living room while he watched *Coronation Street*. My first six was back over his head beyond the far end of the sofa, and my first paternal pieces of advice were 'Never throw your wicket away cheaply' and 'Bowl to your field'. I also remember him saying, 'Cricketers are like cowboys in a gunfight – they only get one chance. If you make a mistake in football, you can come back. In baseball, it's three strikes and you are out. But in cricket, when the finger goes up, that's it. It's a one-ball game.'

Jimmy Irani is not one of those 'the game is the thing' people. He likes to win and he started to bring over professionals to boost Daisy Hill's chances. It worked – they won five championships and had several near-misses while he was in charge. These guys used to become part of the family and some of my first cricket coaching came from Sonny

Ramadhin, the great West Indies spin bowler from the era of Worrell, Walcott and Weekes. Dad would tell me to stand very still by the sight-screen and watch Sonny bowl. 'See if you can spot which way the ball will spin as it leaves his hand.' Dad always wanted me to be a spinner but, as I grew up, I realised it is a skill that is all-consuming and I enjoyed batting, so didn't want to spend all my time mastering the black arts later perfected by the likes of Shane Warne and Phil Tufnell. I also didn't like the idea of being swiped all over the pitch, even though Dad assured me I would pick up a lot of wickets from miss-hits.

Javed Miandad, the Pakistani superstar, was only a teenager when he spent a season in Bolton but he became my idol. That year he scored more than a thousand runs and took over a hundred wickets despite missing the last six games. He lived with us and not only made sure I held the bat correctly, he also buttoned up my blazer and sent me off looking neat and tidy on my first day at school. I worshipped him and from then on I used to comb through the *Cricketer* magazine or the *Benson & Hedges Yearbook* to find out how he'd done. Even when he went on to become one of the greatest ever batsmen and a Pakistan legend, he never forgot my family. I remember when I toured Pakistan with England A, he sought me out and invited me to spend the evening with him and his family.

I'm not sure what Dad would have said if I'd done a Billy Elliott and said I wanted to become a ballet dancer but fortunately the situation never arose because I was sport mad from the start. Every night, I'd race home from school, grab a sandwich that Mum would have ready for me, then dash back out to play with my mates. Whether it was in the genes or all that gilt-edged coaching, I seemed to take to most sports quite easily and I was lucky because I was always taller and stronger than most kids of my age. That probably had something to do with Mum's home cooking and the fact that Dad's 'day job' was in the meat business, which meant we would often have steak for breakfast.

I went to kick-boxing classes, played basketball for the north of England, and had tennis coaching with a guy who reckoned I was like a young Roscoe Tanner because I could hit the ball hard at eight years old. But my two passions were cricket and football. Funnily enough, once I was old enough to start playing in teams, which was around the age of six, football was the sport Dad and I shared most, simply because in the summer we would be playing cricket in different matches.

Football was the main sport at my senior school, Smithills Comprehensive. We had some inspirational teachers in Gary Dickinson, former sprinter Steve Caldwell and Stuart Bowman. It wasn't a job for them: they had real enthusiasm for their sport and loved passing that on to the kids in their charge. They could be tough – if you messed them about they would hang you up on the coat pegs and leave you dangling. They demanded high standards and wouldn't allow us to drop below our best. Steve Caldwell introduced the idea of warming up before football matches. We would line up on the halfway line in our reversible kit – red for home, white away – and he'd have us stretching, running shuttles and doing star jumps. The opposition used to stand on the sidelines taking the piss but, if we dared look over at them, Steve would bark at us to concentrate. We hated it at first because we felt daft but then we found that we would come flying out of the blocks and often have games won before the other kids had got into it.

There were some good players in that team – Kenny Hampson and Glen Foster at the back, Jason Nash, who is now back at the school as a PE teacher and head of year, and little midfielder Sean Atkinson who could dribble for fun and who Dad loved to watch. I played up front, a Norman Whiteside figure, and had some success. The highlight was probably the day I scored seven in a game on my way to more than 40 in a season.

I went to watch my first league match when I was about seven. Dad had several season tickets at Manchester United and decided I was now old enough to be introduced to the glory that is Old Trafford. This might come as a big surprise to those sceptics from the blue side of Manchester, but there were and are a lot of Man United fans living in Lancashire. It became a regular routine – play football on Saturday morning, grab a quick shower, dash home for a bite to eat while watching *Saint & Greavsie* or Bob Wilson on *Football Focus* and then pile into Dad's red van with four or five other fans in the back and head off to the match. We'd park near some warehouses, not far from the ground. Dad always tried to get a good spot to make a quick getaway after the game but, as he would never dream of leaving before the final whistle, it was usually pointless and we ended up in a traffic jam. On the short walk to the ground, we'd stop at Vincent's Italian Ice Cream van to pick up a 99 and then meet up with Dad's friend Kevin Thomas and his family under the Munich clock.

Even though these were not the glamour days at the Theatre of Dreams, I was still wide-eyed. Despite having Lou Macari, Gordon McQueen, Bryan Robson, Ray Wilkins and a young Mark Hughes, United were a workmanlike side who enjoyed a few good cup runs. Mostly the old boys around me talked fondly of the Busby Babes, the tragedy of Munich and the golden era of Charlton, Law and Best. Dad would also tell me about the great players he had seen at Burnley in the 1960s and, if I looked away when Ian St John or Jimmy Greaves were on TV, he'd say, 'Listen to these guys, Ronnie. They were great, great footballers and they know what they are talking about.' One of the biggest thrills for Dad when I played for Essex was finding out that Jimmy is a big cricket fan, and they often sat together, watching matches at Chelmsford. Greavsie's son Danny ran the Essex shop for a while, and my wife Lorraine would help him out some days.

In those days, the average crowd at Old Trafford was around 28,000, so it was always a thrill when you listened to Stuart Hall on *Sports Report* on the way back from a game and heard him tell of 48,000 being 'packed into the ground like red-and-white sardines'. Twice a season – against City and Liverpool – the crowd would be a 58,000 sell-out. These were always extra special occasions, particularly when we won.

As talkSPORT listeners will know, I'm still a Man U fan today, although I like to think that I'm not one-eyed and can appreciate other teams and great players whatever strip they wear. Even though Liverpool were 'the enemy', I still loved watching their great teams on *Match of the Day* and rather wished we had signed players like Kevin Keegan, Ian Rush and Kenny Dalglish. Things started to look up at Old Trafford after Alex Ferguson took over, although I can remember the time when the Stretford Enders were calling for him to be sacked. A good job they didn't get their way! Dad used to watch the reserves as well and told me about a kid to look out for called Ryan Giggs. I saw Steve Bruce make his debut and Gary Pallister arrive and a string of great players like Paul Ince and the incomparable Roy Keane help put the club on the right track. Meanwhile, the youth set-up was discovering talents like David Beckham, Paul Scholes and the Neville brothers, Gary and Phil, who I played cricket against at Greenmount CC.

But for me the most exciting entrance – it was so much more than a mere arrival – I've witnessed while watching United was the day a Frenchman strutted on to the Old Trafford stage, his collar turned up, his chest stuck out as though he owned the place. Eric Cantona had just won the championship with Leeds United and Fergie had snapped him up for a bargain million quid. His presence seemed to instil confidence and self-belief in all the others. He was the catalyst for the breathtaking run of success that followed. He made a great club a great team and so, when Lorraine and I bought a proud-looking Doberman in 1999, he had to have a red collar and was named Eric.

Dad and I hardly ever had the same opportunity to enjoy watching first-class cricket together because of our playing commitments. I can only remember going to see one Lancashire county match before I joined the ground staff and I only watched one Test match as a boy. That was at Old Trafford in 1980. Sonny Ramadhin got us a pair of tickets in the VIP section for England against the West Indies and I turned up clutching my sandwiches in my kung-fu bag. Those were the days of the great West Indian pacemen and I recall Michael Holding taking a run up that seemed to start about two rows in front of where I was sitting. The Windies also had some very talented batsmen, including Clive Lloyd and Viv Richards. England had a few good players too, like Mike Gatting, Geoffrey Boycott and Ian Botham, but the star of the show was a little guy named Malcolm Marshall, who was quite new on the scene. He was only about 5ft 9in – tiny compared to his fellow quickies – but he steamed in, knocked over three quick wickets and caused an England collapse. I was massively impressed. Little did I realise that about 12 years later I would play against him. I only faced one ball, but at least I can say I batted against arguably the greatest fast bowler the world has ever seen.

The first West Indian paceman I ever faced was much more hostile. Franklin Stevenson came over to play for Greenmount in the Bolton League and he relished the uncovered wickets that at times made him almost unplayable. I was already in the Heaton first team and, at the age of 14, found myself watching this giant Barbadian charging towards me. Franklin was noted for his clever use of the slower ball, but I never saw any evidence of it that day. Fourteen or not, I was merely an obstacle to be removed and he tried to bounce the shit out of me from the first ball. I ducked and weaved and let a few fizz past my head. Several more whacked into my ribs and chest, but somehow I survived and gradually found a way of getting bat on ball and went on to score a half-century. We lost the game but such was the spirit at Heaton that the lads bought me a pint of bitter shandy to celebrate my achievement. It was a great feeling to be one of the boys when the rest of the boys were men, although, when I took my shirt off to go to bed that night, my body was blotched purple with bruises.

That reaction was fairly typical of Heaton. They had no money to pay amateurs and only a little for overseas professionals. Former Barbados and Kent all-rounder Hartley Alleyne was probably the biggest name they signed, but he'd already been around the wealthier local clubs before joining Heaton. I remember playing against him in the

Huddersfield League. But if Heaton were seldom among the trophies, they enjoyed their cricket and were genuinely pleased to celebrate a young player's success. They always made youngsters feel welcome and on a Friday night there could be more than a hundred kids playing cricket beneath my bedroom window. Jack Taylor was in charge of the juniors and Jeff Todd was club captain. They loved the fact that I was eager to learn and gave me tremendous encouragement. There was never any question of 'when you get older' – if you were good enough, you were old enough and they threw you in the deep end. I was in the Under-13 side before my seventh birthday and quickly got used to playing against boys much older than me.

Having hung around the dressing room a lot with Dad, I was used to the atmosphere and unbothered by the language. I didn't blink twice when a guy named Phil Roberts, who was built like a tank, started coaching me at the age of 13 and yelled after one particularly bad, cross-bat shot, 'If I ever see you play another shot like that, I'll kick you up the fucking arse, you pillock.' I got the point.

League cricket in Lancashire is an institution. It's hard for people down south to realise just what a big part it plays in life up there. There are clubs all over the place – there must be 40 in the Bolton area alone – and, without wishing to preach, I believe it's important that these leagues are supported. The clubs are great places for youngsters to grow up – there's a nice social side as well as the sport and the whole family can get involved. Cricket clubs are not snobbish like some golf clubs and you don't find the parents yelling obscenities at the officials like you do at a lot of youth football games. I think that most kids that come through the ranks of a cricket club turn out to be all right as people.

Heaton Cricket Club was a great place to be as a teenager because they treated you as an adult as long as you behaved properly. One of my pals, Jason Nash, had a bench and we used to go to his place and do weight training. We were both big lads for 15 and on most Friday nights, dressed in our chinos and blazers – it was the era of Rick Astley after all – we went into town to the Balmoral pub for a few beers and then on to a nightclub called the Ritzy. I'm sure the bouncers knew we were under age but they also knew we wouldn't cause any trouble. Occasionally we'd bump into people from the cricket club and they'd buy us a pint! We'd roll out of the nightclub late and catch the last bus home where I'd let myself in quietly and creep upstairs before Mum and Dad realised what the time was and how much I'd been drinking.

My parents were always very supportive and, even though they didn't have that much spare cash, every birthday and Christmas I would get my football and cricket kit. In the early days I used to borrow bats and pads from the Heaton dressing room, but then I got my own first bat, which remains one of the best presents I ever received. Mum ordered my first gloves and pads from a mail-order catalogue and I can still recall the excitement I felt the day they arrived through the post.

I think I was fortunate in a way that Dad wasn't able to see many of my matches. I was able to perform without worrying what he would say. Even though she didn't enjoy driving that much, Mum used to take me to matches but she never commented on how I'd played, probably just relieved to have negotiated the traffic and found the ground. When I got home, Dad would ask how I'd done and, even if I knew I'd got out to a crap shot, I'd make out I'd been unlucky or been done by a great ball or suffered a terrible umpiring decision.

I knew where I'd gone wrong and there was no point in risking a lecture about 'knuckling down' or 'never give away your wicket'.

Mind you, there was the odd occasion when Dad did watch me and on one memorable day he gave me some match-winning advice. It was a schools cup final and I was captain. I scored a hundred then bowled the first over nice and tight but the lad at the other end got whacked all over the place and went for about 20 runs in one over. I heard a whistle from the boundary and went over to see Dad, who pointed out that my football team-mate Glen Foster, who was our wicketkeeper, was also a good bowler. I took the hint and for the rest of the match I would bowl at one end with Glen keeping wicket, then I'd take the gloves while he bowled. We won the cup but our tactics weren't widely approved of and they changed the rules the following year.

As I worked my way through the age groups, I set a few league records, started to get my name in the local paper and got picked for Lancashire and England schoolboys, taking 6-24 on my international debut against Wales. Through these games I got to know other young players around the country and struck up a firm friendship with another local lad, John Crawley, who was later at Lancashire with me and then in the same England team.

There was only one innings I regret. Heaton were playing against Kearsley where Dad was now in the second team. Their first XI were short of players that day and, even though he was 57 years old, he agreed to play. He bowled against me with a wet ball, which made it hard for him to get any purchase, and I smashed him all round the ground, including two sixes off consecutive balls, one of which broke the slates on our neighbour's roof. It's one of the few things in my life that, if I could take it back, I would. But perhaps his granddaughters will gain revenge for him by spanking me at tennis or golf one day.

From the age of around 14 or 15, I realised that I had to make a decision about my future. If I was going to become a professional sportsman, I would have to concentrate on one sport and not try to be a jack of all trades. Bolton Wanderers, then in the lower divisions, had expressed interest in my becoming an apprentice at Burnden Park and I probably could have made a modest living at that level. But I realised that much of my football success was down to the fact that I was bigger and stronger than the other lads my age and that advantage wouldn't last when I moved up the grades. In cricket, however, I had been playing successfully against men for a while and knew I could handle it. So cricket it was, and nothing could have been more perfect than when Lancashire offered me a contract at the age of 16.

CHAPTER 4

STOP ME IF YOU'RE FEELING FRUITY

I was a month short of my 17th birthday and just finished another good season at Heaton Cricket Club when Lancashire told me to turn up at Old Trafford for the announcement of my signing. I was impressed, thinking they must rate me pretty highly to hold a press conference. It was only when I got there that I realised the main point of calling the journalists together was to let the world know that they had signed England all-rounder Phil de Freitas. The boys from the national newspapers didn't take much notice of me, but I got reasonable coverage in the local papers and the following day I made my debut for the Lancashire second team against Glamorgan at Old Trafford to round off a good summer.

The signing of de Freitas was a sign that Lancashire were ambitious to win trophies and were assembling a great squad of players. They already had Mike Watkinson as an all-rounder so I realised it would be hard for me to break into the first team, but I was always ready to back myself and to put in the work that was necessary to make it. From now on cricket was to be my number-one priority and I played a hell of a lot of matches the following season, despite the fact there was a new distraction in my life in the form of a stunning-looking girl with legs to kill for.

By this time, Dad had arranged my first non-cricket job, working part-time at Tom Fraser's butcher's shop. Tom taught me to bone brisket, grind mince and make sausages, but the job was somewhat lacking in glamour so after three months I moved on. I took up an offer to work in a video store owned by Fil Mercer – he insists on the F because he says it's easier to spell and that people remember an unusual name. He is one of several brothers well known in Bolton, and indeed further afield, for their entrepreneurial leanings. I went on to work with several of them over the years, with varying degrees of success.

The video shop suited me down to the ground – there was less blood, a bit more money and I'd always liked movies. As a kid I was hooked on the *Rocky* films and, even though they are a bit cheesy towards the end of the series, they still strike a chord with me today. I identified with the strangely satisfying pain of pushing yourself to your absolute limits in training, the rush you get when you realise that your body has just been stronger or gone faster than ever before, the pleasurable ache of achievement. I can remember the first thrill of watching the scene in *Rocky II* where Sylvester Stallone comes out of his house in the mean streets of Philadelphia to a fanfare of horns that build into Bill Conti's uplifting 'Rocky Theme' as our hero jogs up the railway line, through the market and then into the city, gradually picking up a trail of kids like a latter-day pied piper until he reaches the top of the steps of the Museum of Art where they all gather round, chanting his name. I wanted to be up there with him. It still makes the short hairs on the back of my neck stand up whenever I see it and I defy anyone to watch it and not feel they could go out and become champion of the world.

I've always been chatty – some would say that was an understatement – and I enjoyed helping customers pick out a film, although I tended to be stronger on action than romance. 'If they ask your opinion, tell them the truth,' Fil advised me. 'If it's crap, tell them it's crap. But, if they don't ask, let them find out for themselves.'

One Sunday night, this terrific-looking girl with a great smile came in to return a video. She had all the right bits in all the right places and, being a leg man, I immediately noticed that she had two of the finest-shaped calves I'd ever seen. Her bum wasn't bad either. It was obvious she knew Vicky Burke, the girl I worked with, so after she'd gone I asked who she was.

'That's Lorraine Chapman. Why? Do you fancy her?'

I admitted I was interested and it was arranged that I would 'bump into' the two of them in the pub the following Friday night. Lorraine and I got on well. We seemed to click straight away – something to do with my sophisticated charm and great patter, I thought. Much later, she told me that, without knowing it, I'd done all the right things to impress her: I'd turned down a cigarette because I didn't smoke, I'd talked about her as much as I'd talked about me, and the clincher was when she asked for a glass of coke I didn't try to persuade her to 'have a real drink' so I could get her pissed. Strangely, no mention of the pop-star looks and the great taste in clothes.

The evening went very well and, as she put on her coat to leave, I said, 'Just a minute. I want to see you again. What's your phone number?'

'I'm not on the phone,' she said, and started to walk away.

My heart sank. I thought she was giving me a line just to put me off but then she turned back and said, 'But my granddad is. He only lives down our street. You can phone me there if you like.'

So I did. I got through to granddad Bill and, a little bit embarrassed, explained who I was and asked if he would please go and get Lorraine. 'Right, lad, just a minute,' he said and I heard him put the phone down, shuffle down his hall, open the front door and leave. I must have hung on for a good couple of minutes and I was beginning to think it was a wind-up when I heard some lighter footsteps running back in and a slightly out-of-breath Lorraine said, 'Hello, Ronnie, is that you?' And that was that. We were, as they say in those parts, courting. We are still together 20 years later, although communication is much easier now they've invented mobile phones.

I soon got to know Lorraine's family, who were having quite a tough time. She had a brother Paul and sister Alison. Her dad wasn't living with them and her mum Pat was holding down three jobs to look after her kids. Lorraine, who was only 16 when I met her, was also grafting to pay her way, getting up at 5.30 each morning to catch the bus to her job as a machinist, making curtains at Dorma for Marks & Spencer.

On one of our first dates, I told her that, as well as working in the video shop, I also played cricket, although, not wanting to sound boastful, I didn't say I was on the books at Lancashire. Lorraine showed a suitable amount of interest and then said, 'I play rounders.' So, being a modern man who likes to share interests – and relishing the idea of seeing those legs in a really short skirt – I went along to watch her and she was pretty good. The match was quite tight and the opposition were getting a bit feisty, so I started to wind them up from the sidelines. It worked in so far as they lost their composure and Lorraine's side won the match but I hadn't realised that women tend to react to losing far more aggressively than men. I couldn't believe it. One woman lost it all together. She picked up first base and threatened to use it as a spear. It was riveting to watch but I decided it was time to make a tactical retreat. I've faced some of the most hostile fast bowlers in the world, but none of them was as scary as that woman and I decided there and then that men should steer well clear when women start scrapping.

It was only when the season started and I began to disappear for weeks on end that Lorraine realised that cricket was my main job. It brought a big change in our lives because we weren't able to see nearly as much of each other, but she never complained once and has always accepted the fact that my work meant we've had to spend long periods apart.

As well as playing for Lancashire second team and Under-25s, I signed for Eagley Cricket Club and so became the youngest ever Bolton League club professional. I also had the chance to play a couple of games up at Penrith, which turned out to be one of the most significant trips in my life. I got chatting to their pro Gavin Murgatroyd – I was filling in while he was injured – and he suggested I should ring a chap he knew called John Bird. 'He's a great bloke – a director of Tesco and a cricket nut. You'll like him.' It was one of the best bits of advice I ever received and was soon to help me in my latest business venture, with Fil Mercer.

Fil – a cross between Arthur Daley and Del Boy with a bit of Alan Sugar thrown in – had sold his video shops to Video World which later became Blockbuster. He was now looking for a new venture to invest in and I was keen to have another string to my bow just in case the cricket didn't work out. He'd assisted in a fruit and veg shop when he was a teenager and reckoned, if modern retail techniques were applied to what was a very old-fashioned business, we could clean up. 'The first thing that has to go is that imitation grass draped over apple boxes,' he said.

We drove all over the north of England, looking at greengrocers and most of them were rubbish. We found a great shop in Sheffield, Arthur Fox Fruiterers, and that gave us several ideas for our own place. Fil put in £75,000 and I borrowed 25 grand off my dad and we started to look for our first shop. We realised that position was everything and, contrary to most advice, we decided our shop should be as close as possible to a big supermarket so we were within walking distance of their car park. We labelled our produce as farm fresh, while everyone believed the supermarket stuff was mass-produced and pre-packaged. It was bollocks because it often came from the same market but it worked for us.

I was determined to be hands-on so I needed a quick education in retailing and that's when I remembered Gavin's tip about John Bird. Surely the Head of Retail at Tesco, a guy employing more than 60,000 people, would be able to put me right? I rang and spoke to his secretary, and a couple of days later he phoned me back and agreed to meet. I warmed to him straight away and he was very encouraging. He even created a training course for me and sent me to work at Tesco's Hatfield branch under the experienced guidance of manager Gary Snell. It was quite an eye-opener. Gary gave me a crash course in everything from rotating stock to display, from margins and profit and loss to how to get customers flowing through the store. He also put me to work in the fruit and veg and dairy sections.

One day, I was on the till when the tannoy sounded out: 'Mrs Robinson to reception, please. Mrs Robinson to reception urgently.'

Gary came racing over and said, 'Quick! That's the code for someone nicking stuff.'

As he spoke, a guy came tearing past me clutching a couple of bottles of whisky, raced out of the door and started to leg it across the car park. For some reason, I went after him. I passed Gary, already puffing, in the car park and set off up the hill towards a roundabout. As I overtook the rather portly security guard, I heard him wheeze, 'Go on, my son! You can get him.'

I was now closing in on the guy and suddenly realised what I was doing. For all I knew, he had a knife. Or even a gun. He'd certainly got a couple of bottles he could break and try to glass me. I kept chasing but made up my mind if it turned nasty I wasn't going to risk my cricket career for a couple of bottles of scotch. I reached out, grabbed his collar and he stopped, clearly knackered and in no state to fight. 'All right, all right,' he panted and put the bottles down. Then he started to walk away.

'Hey, mate!' I shouted to him. 'You've got to stay here! Don't make it difficult. I don't want to roll around the floor with you, but I'll stop you if I have to.'

He stopped and at that moment the security guard and a couple of members of staff caught us up and to my amazement jumped on him and pinned him to the floor.

As we walked back down the hill, I said to Gary, 'Is it always like this?'

'Oh yeah,' he said. 'At least one a week.'

Shortly after that, I had to fill in one of those questionnaires sports people get from newspapers and magazines. One of the questions was: What do you do in the off season? I wrote: 'Security guard, Tesco'.

By the time I got back home bursting with ideas, Fil had found our first shop and we kitted it out like no greengrocers Bolton had ever seen. We tiled the floor, made an inviting wide entrance, fixed up a television to create a bit of interest and installed a machine for making freshly squeezed orange juice. As far as I know, it was the first in any greengrocers in the country and it brought in loads of customers. I would stand there, squeeze the oranges and hand round samples. 'Here you are, luv, try this. The freshest orange juice in the world.' Then I'd bottle it in front of them. Another satisfied customer. We also bought a van and had the slogan painted on the side: 'Stop me if you're feeling fruity!'

Fil and I worked our socks off. We'd be in the market at 2.30am to buy the produce and we wouldn't finish until about half past six that night. Lorraine thought I was a gentleman because I didn't try it on with her but in reality I was too knackered.

But the shop took off. We ploughed all the money back into the business and soon we had three shops. Fil was a great partner and knew a hell of a lot about business, which he was happy to pass on to me. There was a lot to learn, some of it making no sense at all, such as the morning a load of retailers were scrambling around the wholesale market desperate to buy some Marks & Spencer reject cauliflowers. 'Why would we buy someone else's cast-offs?' I asked, completely bewildered.

'Because they are still quality at a slightly knock-down price and you can sell them as M&S collies.'

I still didn't get it but put in a bid anyway.

Fil could be a hard bastard if he thought I'd got it wrong. There were several bitterly cold mornings, well before dawn, when I would get a bollocking because I'd bought the wrong gear, maybe the 10p lemons when I should have bought those at 3p. It wasn't easy to take because I was usually dog tired but I knew he was only doing it for my own good, so I bit my tongue.

It was on one of those early-morning sessions at the market that I spotted the former Lancashire captain Jack Bond driving a wagon for Liptrots, a well-known local firm. I'd grown up hearing stories about Jack. He was a Lancashire legend – he'd taken an under-performing team and won the one-day Sunday League two years on the trot and followed that with three successive Gillette Cup final victories at Lord's. I'd also come across him as an umpire and knew him to be a lovely bloke and a fair umpire. I was taken aback that someone as well known and successful as Jack Bond could be driving a wagon for a living at an unearthly hour of the morning. It gave me a new outlook on fame.

At the start of my second season with Lancashire, I returned to Heaton as their pro and I also had a season among the Yorkies with Skelmanthorpe in the Huddersfield League. My life was manic – I'd play all week with Lancashire then Saturday and Sunday with the club sides, who expected me to bowl my full 25 overs and open the batting. Fortunately, I was as strong as an ox but there is no doubt it took a toll on my body and was probably the starting point for some of the injuries I suffered later on. I was already walking with a limp but I disguised it because I didn't want to stop: playing cricket seven days a week was my idea of paradise and everything seemed to be going my way.

At the end of my first season at Lancashire, I was selected to tour Australia with the England Under-19 side. I was one of the youngest in the squad and only played a couple of one-day games but it introduced me to the management of Graham Saville and was the start of a relationship that was to prove pivotal in my career. The following summer I was selected for the U19s again, to play against Pakistan at the Oval, and was due to travel on the tour to New Zealand that autumn but had to withdraw because of a knee injury which required an operation, the first of many during my career.

I'd also made my Lancashire first-team debut against the Zimbabwe touring side and was about to taste my first major international success.

CHAPTER 5
CHIRPING GOD

Not many batsmen boast about getting out but I was once run out by Vivian Richards – not yet knighted but already a god. It was my competitive one-day debut in Lancashire's first team and a match I will never forget.

I'd been given the nod to play against Glamorgan and got to Old Trafford very early to warm up well. As I was walking back to the pavilion, I saw the man I'd grown up worshipping standing near the entrance. Isaac Vivian Alexander Richards was in his early forties, past his prime but still a legend and I was going to play against him. I walked towards the dressing room, head down, too in awe to say a word. As I passed him, I heard that deep Caribbean voice so familiar from countless TV interviews.

'Ronnie Irani.'

I was shocked he knew my name. I turned back and muttered, 'Mr Richards.'

He laughed. 'Just call me Viv.'

'Err, right, Viv, sir.' I don't think I'd ever been so nervous.

'You're making your debut today?'

'Yes, sir.'

'Well, good luck and good luck for the rest of your career.'

Viv Richards, one of the greatest men ever to grace the game of cricket, had taken the time not just to notice me but to wish me well. That was fucking massive. I bounced up the steps to the dressing room and vowed there and then that, if I ever got to be a tenth of the player he was, I would seek out kids making their way in the game and give them a bit of a gee-up.

Once we crossed the boundary rope, his attitude was less benevolent. It was my own fault. For some insane reason, I decided I would take a quick single to one of the finest-ever fielders. The odds were in my favour – he wasn't young any more and the ball took a nasty bobble just before it reached him – but he still managed to swoop and throw in one graceful movement and I heard the clatter of the stumps with the safety of the crease still yards away. As I trudged off I cursed myself: 'What on earth were you thinking of? You've watched him all your life. You've learned from him. You know how he fields. You're a tosser.'

While I was totally in awe of the man, I was also fighting for my career, so, when it came time to bowl against him, I backed myself and took him on. I sent down one particularly good ball and he tried to knock it out of the ground. It was the last ball of the over and I walked towards him and said, 'What are you doing have a whoosh at that? You should respect me when I bowl a good ball at you.' I turned on my heel and started back towards the umpire to collect my sweater, already regretting what I'd said.

I heard that voice again: 'Young man.'

I ignored him. The umpire handed me my sweater and said, 'He'll kill you next over.'

'Young man. Young man.' The voice was a bit more insistent and a bit closer.

I decided to pretend I'd not heard him and walked away towards the boundary.

'YOUNG MAN!'

No pretending I hadn't heard that. I'll have to face him and take my bollocking, I thought, cursing myself for being an idiot. I turned. The great Viv Richards had followed me beyond the umpire at the bowler's end and was still coming.

'Yes, Viv. What is it?'

'Young man, you will go far in the game.' And with that he turned and went back to his crease.

He blocked every ball of my next over for a maiden and at the end of it said, 'Well bowled.'

The crowd could sense something was going on and applauded. I think they loved the fact that I was willing to take him on. My team-mates weren't so enthusiastic. Some of them had already made it clear they thought I was too full of myself and would do better to keep my mouth buttoned. They thought a rookie should show more deference and when we got back in the dressing room a few started taking the piss, accusing me of being a big-time charlie, chirping Viv Richards. Dexter Fitton, my pal from the second team, congratulated me and John Stanworth, the second-team player-coach, said, 'Ignore that lot. That was good out there.'

But I was still feeling low and reluctantly put on my blazer and tie and made my way to the small committee room where players from both sides have a drink after the game.

As I opened the door, it was just my luck that the person standing next to the bar was Viv Richards. I froze for a moment. What do I do now? I couldn't turn round and go back, and I couldn't pretend I didn't drink.

He spotted me and said, 'What do you want to drink, Ronnie? Have a rum and coke.' He ordered the drink and added, 'Well done out there today. You taking me on – that's what you've got to do every day. When you are out there, you have to fight for everything. Don't give an inch.'

'Thanks,' I said. 'I've had a bit of a bagging from my team-mates about it. I didn't mean to be disrespectful.' I paused and blurted out, 'Did you mean it when you said I'll go far?'

'I meant it. I'm going to watch out for you. Ignore people who are negative. But also remember, if you take someone on in a match, try to shake hands with them afterwards. If they won't have a beer with you, it's their problem, not yours, but you should make the effort.'

I spent the next hour in the great man's company, loving just being able to listen to him talk about cricket. As he got up to go, he said, 'Do you need a lift somewhere?'

'No, it's all right. My mum and dad are waiting for me.'

He chuckled. 'You are a young lad, aren't you?'

I never forgot that day. I didn't see him again until 2008 when we hooked up to do four dinners in as many nights, four of the best nights of my life. I'd learned a lot about cricket from watching Viv on TV as a kid but he also taught me about being a professional sportsman, what it means on and off the field of play. Superstar is an overused word in modern life but he truly was one in every respect and I just wish some of today's sports people carried themselves with as much dignity and sheer class as he does.

I've got no time for people who think that, because they have a talent, it gives them a licence to act as they please and feel no need to put something back. I remember Tommy Smith, a key part of that great Liverpool football era, telling me that, when he was trying to raise funds for some of the older Anfield players who had fallen on hard times, a few of the current side refused to sign shirts because they were being sold. I've heard of clubs stopping players signing photographs because they were being auctioned on eBay. So what? Football and footballers make enough out of the game. Does it matter if someone else makes a few quid out of a photo? Some of them need a reality check.

Back in Bolton, the greengrocery business was doing well but then along came the recession of the early 1990s. We got through the summer OK because there is a good margin on soft fruits but then we struggled. It's hard to make a living out of spuds and carrots. Fil tried to reassure me that things would turn round but I was worried about finding myself lumbered with a load of debt and knew I couldn't afford that kind of distraction at this stage of my career. So we agreed that I would leave my money in the business but would sign it all over to him. Fil finally sold the shops and eventually paid me back my £25,000 out of his other businesses, which was an incredibly honourable thing to do. It had been a massive learning experience for me and I would apply some of the lessons when I again went into business with the Mercer family later in my career.

Life as a young professional at Lancashire was a strange mixture of emotions. I loved my cricket, and the bunch of guys I was with in the second team was terrific – the spirit and camaraderie in that group were as good as I've ever experienced. But there was also growing frustration. I became aware that my first-team chances were going to be few and far between. That was partly because there were some very good players ahead of me and I had no argument with that, but there was more to it than that. There was a divide between the first and second teams, right down to capped players changing in a different room from uncapped ones, even when they were playing in the same match. We put a sign on the second-team dressing-room door that read 'MUSHROOMS' and, when one of our senior colleagues asked what it was about, we explained it was because we were kept in the dark and had shit shovelled on us from time to time.

I also felt there was a lot of snobbery in the club, with people like Mike Atherton, who came from the posh part of Lancashire and was educated at Cambridge, looking down on oiks from Bolton like me, people who had too much to say for themselves and didn't know their place. I sensed that, for me to make it, I would have to work a lot harder than most people. It was a challenge I needed to face up to. It was no good whingeing and moaning that it was unfair. That would just confirm what people were thinking. So I buckled down and worked even harder. I was determined I wouldn't let them grind me down and vowed never to let them see a moment's doubt. I kept on smiling, even when I felt low. I kept on offering my opinions – partly because I knew it annoyed them but partly because I'd grown up in dressing rooms where everyone's view counted and I thought that's how it should be. I'm a great believer in saying what you have to say to someone's face and then moving on.

It wasn't all negative. I received terrific support and encouragement from those in charge of the second team, people like John Savage, Alan Ormrod, the Lancashire manager, and ironically, in view of my later experiences with England, the coach David Lloyd. Bumble, as he was known throughout cricket, was a chirpy character and his enthusiasm for the game was infectious. He would hand out bollockings when he thought they were due but mostly his criticisms were constructive. I remember working on my game with him and thinking he's a top man. He also seemed to rate me, which made his change of heart later in my career even more puzzling.

I was doing well on the field. The highlight was the double hundred I scored for the second team against a Kent attack that included England bowler Richard Ellison, Min Patel and a guy named Duncan Spencer who was seriously quick. His bowling was once timed at 98mph but he was later banned from the game when it turned out he'd been taking steroids.

My cricket education increased when I was introduced to the joys of reverse swing by one of the masters of the art. I don't want to get too technical but, for those of you who are not familiar with this magical weapon in the bowler's armoury, it is the ball the batsman expects to move out towards the slips but which cuts sharply back and rattles his stumps. Pakistani bowlers discovered it with devastating results. If you want to see some perplexed expressions on batsmen's faces, go on YouTube and call up reverse swing. It's the stuff bowlers' dreams are made of.

Wasim Akram was one of the best in the world at what was then called late swing. He was Lancashire's star bowler when I was at Old Trafford and I think Javed Miandad had asked him to look out for me, because he was always helpful from the day I joined the ground staff. He was a great role model for any wannabe bowler, not just technically sound but with a massive heart. He struggled against injury but time after time he would shrug it off and keep powering in. All fast bowlers bowl through pain – if they don't, they won't play much cricket – but this guy was special. I have seen Wasim steam in without wilting when I've known he should be on the treatment table. Even when he was only 90 per cent fit, he was a better bowler than almost anyone else out there.

It was on one of his appearances in the second team, on his way back after an injury, that he handed me a key to bowling glory. Different bowlers have different targets in their mind when they run in – some aim for a spot on the pitch, others concentrate on the stumps but I have always visualised the ball flying past the edge of the bat. If the batsman misses, I've got a chance of lbw or bowled; if he just makes contact, it could carry to the keeper or slips. That's what I had in mind in this game as the ball started to move around. I ran in and let go of a peach of a delivery, but, instead of beating the bat on the off side, it shot down the leg side for byes. I was confused. What had I done wrong? The same thing happened to the next ball and I started to panic inside. Had I lost the ability to swing the ball? What should I do next?

Wasim came running down the pitch as I walked back to my mark. 'Ronnie, hold the ball exactly as you would for an outswinger but pitch it six to eight inches outside off stump and let it go as fast as you can,' he said.

Now I was really bemused. Everything I knew about bowling told me that if I followed his advice I would bowl a wide. But who was I to argue with Wasim?

I ran in and zipped one down the off side. Instead of swinging away, it cut back sharply, beat the batsman and almost took his off peg. Wow! The next over I sent one down that completely bamboozled the batsman and trapped him plumb lbw.

As we gathered in a huddle, Wasim said, 'Well done, you've got it.'

I wasn't sure what it was that I'd got, but I knew it was

important. I'd never been blessed with tremendous pace but now I'd got something even more lethal.

I gradually learned that the reason the ball behaves in that extraordinary way is the contrast between the shiny side, which you keep polishing, and the other side which has been roughened up through play. You are allowed to use spit or sweat to shine the ball but you are not supposed to do anything to rough up the other side. I soon found out that plenty of bowlers were using a thumbnail to 'assist' what was happening naturally and I confess that from time to time I joined them. I felt, if we were getting turned over by this tactic, I would use it to my team's advantage too.

Some will say that I cheated but I would argue that I was only pushing the laws to their limit just as others did in their own way. If the odd nail should happen to roughen up one side of the ball a little, is that any more reprehensible than the people who discovered that the ball would shine like never before if you sucked a pepermint when you spat on it? And what about those clubs who prepare a wicket that is so flat you could bowl on it all day and get no help at all? They are all cheating in a way, but to me they are just pushing their advantage as hard as they can.

At that time, umpires seemed unaware that a certain amount of ball-roughing was going on. They were only looking for old-style seam-picking, when bowlers used their fingernails to raise the seam, which increases grip and gets the ball to move. I recall toiling away on a flat pitch that was giving the bowlers no help at all in a game that was petering out into a high-scoring draw when the umpire at my end, a former fast bowler, said, 'Come on, lad, get the seam up.' I did and took three wickets.

I never felt uncomfortable giving the rough side of the ball a bit of a helping hand, despite the clear disapproval of Graham Gooch at Essex. He had a batsman's natural hatred of reverse swing, and would make a point of ostentatiously showing the ball to the other slip fielders to demonstrate what I was doing. A few batsmen murmured, 'Fucking cheat,' when they trailed off having failed to deal with a great delivery, but that always seemed like sour grapes to me. I've been on the other end of reverse swing many times and never complained when it got me out. I was of the Hansie Cronje school on this. I knocked over his stumps with one that boomeranged. He was in his prime then, and he was a great batsman. He just looked down the wicket, nodded and said, 'Well bowled, great skills.'

Hansie was caught up in the 2000 match-fixing scandal linked to gambling in the sub-continent. As a member of the England team at the time, I was given a briefing by Scotland Yard about how the system worked. I was gobsmacked by how simple it was. The police warned us that the bookies would 'groom' us by just being friendly at first and then giving presents. When the relationship was reasonably good, they would ask for simple information like news on an injured player or the weather conditions, all of which seemed quite innocent, although relevant if you were setting spread-betting odds. Finally, they would drag you in so deep that it would be difficult to claw your way out. Fortunately, I've never been approached – they probably knew they would get sent away with a flea in their ear – but like most cricketers I've seen some bizarre run-outs that have made me wonder what was going on.

The extra wickets I started to take thanks to Wasim and my continuing success with the bat meant Graham Saville was still picking me for England U19s, and in the summer of 1991 I enjoyed a memorable series against a very good

Australian team. The first one-day match was my debut at Lord's, where every cricketer in the world wants to play. I rang John Bird and told him I'd been picked and he said, 'Great! I'll see you there. We've got a box at Lord's.'

The Aussies were a talented outfit – when are they not? – and their side included people like their captain Damien Martyn, Greg Blewett, Adam Gilchrist and Michael Kasprowicz. They made a big score and we were facing a tough ask. John Crawley got some runs and when I went in we needed to push on. I smashed 38 off around 20 balls, including a six into John's Tesco box. He and his guests were out on the balcony waving their arms enthusiastically, which was a strange sight in a ground that was nearly empty and where his was the only executive box in use.

I had several good knocks in that series, including 56 at Chelmsford where John was also in attendance, and it culminated in my first international century, 106 not out, in front of my own members at Old Trafford. I was voted player of the series and Graham Saville went out of his way to congratulate me.

Everyone at Lancashire was very complimentary, but I still hardly got a sniff of the first team. Neil Fairbrother had taken over as captain from David Hughes and he was struggling in the role. He wasn't my biggest fan and only picked me a couple of times. Funnily enough, we get on better now than we did then and I tend to pull his leg and thank him for not picking me because it helped to plant the seed that I should move elsewhere.

I didn't have anything other than club cricket to compare my situation to, and I found life at Lancashire a long way from the spirit that existed at Heaton. I was starting to realise that, while cricket is a team game, at the top level it can also be very much an individual sport. Bowlers need others to take catches, batsmen need someone at the other end to take runs, and we all rely on our team-mates to do their bit in the field, but, when it comes down to it, everyone is looking after number one. I wasn't alone in the second team of that era in feeling the frustration of not getting a chance no matter how well we performed. Driving back from a match, David Lloyd's son Graham told me he was getting a hard time from one of the senior pros but added, 'Don't worry, Ronnie – I'll have the bastard's job one day.'

I realised he was right. From that moment on, every time one of my senior colleagues tried to put me down, I'd just smile and say to myself, 'I know why you don't want me to succeed – you're scared I'm going to take your job. Well, that's just what I'm going to do. You might think you're snuffing out the flame, but you are just fanning it brighter and hotter.'

You need the hide of a rhinoceros in any dressing room or you won't survive. People are not shy with their comments and criticisms and even the banter, which seems light-hearted, can have cruel barb in it. But at times Lancashire went beyond that. There was abuse that amounted to bullying and, if you didn't stand up to it, you could easily go under. I vividly remember the day John Crawley decided he'd had enough. John is the most mild mannered of men and great company, so his outburst came as something of a shock to everyone. He'd been waiting some time for a game of snooker and, just as he was about to rack up the balls, a so-called senior player told him to move aside because he wanted to play. That was it. Frustration that had been bubbling up over the months erupted. John took his snooker cue and whacked the guy. No one messed with John after that.

My own reputation as someone to leave alone came after a night out in Bury with Nick Derbyshire and a couple of other guys from the ground staff. Nick, the brother of BBC 5 live's Victoria Derbyshire, was always great company and we used to drive around the country to matches together. He was a great athlete and a fine fast bowler, and we became firm friends when we spent a winter playing club cricket in South Africa. We stayed with relatives of his, Geoffrey and Janet Bentham, in their magnificent house in Durban. When we weren't playing cricket, we would go to the gym and then on to the beach to show off our finely honed bodies.

Although he was one of the lads, Nick suffered from reverse snobbery – some people took exception to the posh accent he'd picked up at school in Ampleforth. I could tell it might be a problem in that Bury pub when we started to get some dirty looks. It was my turn to drive so I wasn't drinking and, as the evening wore on, I sensed the hostility growing, even though we were minding our own business and weren't being loud. When the landlord called time, I suggested we drank up and got out sharpish.

We all climbed into the car we'd borrowed from one of the guys' mothers and I started to ease out of the car park, only to find my way blocked by a gang of about 15 lads. I decided to keep going gently and hope they would part. One of them smacked his hand against the windscreen in front of me, then another took something harder to a rear-side window and smashed it. That pissed me off and I said, 'That's it.'

The other three echoed, 'Yeah, that's it,' and we all climbed out, four fit young cricketers, facing odds of nearly four to one. In fact, they were worse than that because I was the only one who could fight.

My martial arts training had taught me to keep out of

fights whenever I could, but this wasn't one I could walk away from.

'Who the fuck broke that window?' I challenged.

A group of blokes came towards me. I took one of them down and smacked another. By now two more had jumped on my back. One of them hit me and I felt my jaw go. I glanced across and saw my mates scuffling with some of the others. I thought, We are going to get battered here.

One guy said, 'I broke your poncy window! What are you going to do about it?'

With two still clinging to my back, I grabbed him and pushed him halfway over a wall and gave him a smack.

A woman's voice yelled, 'Stop it! Stop it!' She started to have a go at me but I interrupted her: 'Don't give me a hard time! We just came for a quiet drink and this lot jumped us. They smashed up my mate's car and all for no reason. You should be having a go at them!' With that we got back in the car and drove off.

We got the window fixed the next morning before the mum spotted the damage and I heard that the guy I'd hit wasn't too badly hurt. I was a bit concerned that Lancashire might take action against me for fighting but nothing was said. Word certainly got back to the dressing room, though, because I noticed a marked reduction in the verbals after that.

Nevertheless, I was beginning to think that hanging around Lancashire wasn't going to fulfil my ambition of regular county cricket. Maybe I should forget my dream of representing my home county and think of moving elsewhere.

CHAPTER 6

MY PAL, THE WANNABE PORN STAR

Dexter Fitton had had enough. He let the shower pour over him and said, 'Ronnie, you've got to fuck off out of here before they grind you down. You can make it. You've got the ability.'

I knew he was right and said, 'What about you?'

He soaped his manhood and smiled. 'I think I'll become a porn star.'

I burst out laughing. 'Well, I don't know about your acting ability but you've certainly got the tackle for it!'

Dex was a quality off-spinner who could smack it about a bit with the bat. He was a genuine guy and one of the best people you could ever want in the dressing room but, with Jack Simmons playing on, he seldom got his chance to show what he could do on the big stage. He realised he should have left the club a few seasons before and now regretted that he'd rejected an offer from Derbyshire in the hope of making the breakthrough at Old Trafford.

He was not alone. Ian Folley from Burnley was tipped as a future England left-arm spinner. He went out of his way to help me and often drove me to and from matches, entertaining me with a mixture of advice and Tracy Chapman tracks. His favourite was 'Talking 'bout a Revolution' and we were often ready to rise up and get our share. Ian had enjoyed a taste of the first team but had got the yips and been dropped down the pecking order, and now he felt quite bitter. Eventually he left and after a couple of years at Derbyshire went to play club cricket in the Lake District.

In a way, our shared frustration created a great spirit in the Lancashire second-team dressing room. We were all in it together, us against the world or rather us against the bastards next door who were standing in our way.

We all believed, if we could get a run in the first team, we could perform. Don't get the impression we were a lot of upstarts with a bloated opinion of ourselves. That team included people who went on to play for England, such as Peter Martin, a Yorkie who liked a swig of Baileys during a game, John Crawley and Graham Lloyd. Then there was Jason Gallian, Nick Speak, Steve Titchard, Nick Derbyshire, Marcus Sharp, Ian Austin, Glen Chapple, Mark Crawley, Jonathan 'Trigger' Fielding and Tim Orrell, whose after-match drink was a pint of white wine and soda. Every one of them could play but promoting young players was not the Lancashire way. I remember having a good match to help us win the semi-final of the Baines Clarkson trophy, a tin-pot second-team competition, but they dropped me for the final and put a senior player in 'because we want to win it'. I felt like screaming but, as the man said, what doesn't break you makes you, so I bit my tongue and made up my mind that one day I would show them.

We took every chance we were given to stake our claim. There were two particularly satisfying pre-season matches when we went head to head with the first team. In theory they should have battered us but in the first clash at Centurion Park in South Africa they scraped victory off the last ball when I bust a gut to try to reach a huge skier but couldn't quite get to it. On the team bus on our way back to the hotel, ex-England opener and Lancashire stalwart Graeme Fowler said, 'You lot took that a bit serious, didn't you?' Of all the senior players, 'Foxy' was probably the one who treated us best, but even he clearly believed places in the team were set and there was no room for others to break in. Some of the players at Lancashire had earned the right to expect their name would be on every team sheet but not all of them, otherwise why have a second team? The second game was back at Old Trafford and we creamed them. They were not happy with us but I don't think they really gave a shit because they knew it wouldn't count for anything once the season got under way.

Towards the end of 1993, I'd been on the ground staff five years and played just nine first-class matches, including against the Zimbabwe tourists and Oxford University. When I'd played in the England U19s, several of my team-mates were already regulars in the county championship game whereas I was in danger of spending my whole career in the stiffs and disappearing off the radar.

I felt I had to move on and would have liked the chance to discuss it with some of the senior players, but Neil Fairbrother had problems of his own as he was just about to pack in the captaincy and I didn't feel confident approaching the others. One day I came across Mike Atherton alone in the dressing room reading the paper. He had just been appointed England captain and, as I'd known him since I was 14, I thought this might be an opportunity to get some advice. He lowered his paper slightly as I came in, glanced at me and said, 'So we're thinking of leaving, are we?'

I said, 'Yeah, there's some great players here and I'm obviously going to struggle to get in the team, so a move might be good for my career. I'm not really sure at the moment.'

He said, 'That's what they all say. We'll see,' and went back to reading his paper. He clearly didn't give a damn and I just thought, You arrogant twat. That's typical of the senior people at this club – no one gives a toss about anyone else.

It was another nudge towards the exit. The only problem was, where could I go? I put out a few feelers and heard on the grapevine that Durham were definitely keen and that Steve Oldham would like to talk to me at Yorkshire. I liked Steve and a move to Yorkshire to team up with Darren Gough sounded attractive, but so far it was all rumour. I was in turmoil. This was a big step, and would things really be any different somewhere else? It was an agonising period and many nights I cried myself to sleep, not sure what to do for the best. Perhaps I'd be daft to jump ship before I knew what Lancashire had in mind for me.

Then the day came when the management summoned the second team to Old Trafford to hear about new contracts. It wasn't the best of days to choose because we had all been shocked to hear that Ian Folley had died at the age of 30. He had got a top edge playing club cricket and the ball had smacked him in the eye. He'd gone in for an operation but suffered a heart attack on the operating table. The contract meeting was held a few hours before a group of us were due to go to his funeral.

We all sat around in the stiffs' dressing room ready to be called into the captain's room next door. I felt very uncomfortable. These were my mates. We'd sweated blood together, enjoyed each other's good times and commiserated when things hadn't gone so well. We'd played hard and occasionally we'd partied hard. We were a team. One reason we had managed to beat the first XI in pre-season was that they played as individuals while we played for each other. But we knew as we sat there, heads down, hardly speaking, that some of us wouldn't be offered a contract to come back next season.

One by one we went in to see team manager David Hughes and chief executive John Brewer. As each one returned the ritual was the same.

'All right?'

'Yeah.'

'Congratulations, mate.'

I was dreading the first one to come back and say no. When it happened, we didn't have to ask the question. Dexter Fitton, the life and soul of the dressing room, came through the door red-faced and obviously choked up. No one said a word. He was our man, but none of us could think of anything to say. He grabbed a black bin-bag and started to empty his locker. Then he slammed it shut and said, 'That's it, lads. I'm done.' That afternoon he carried Ian Folley's coffin.

A few more of the lads were given the bad news before it was my turn to go in. Part of me hoped they would tell me I wasn't being retained. I didn't want to go back and say I was OK because it would seem as though I was rubbing my mates' faces in it. David Hughes and John Brewer were all smiles as I walked into the room, almost as though they didn't realise what they were doing to people's lives.

I was feeling quite emotional and only half took in what they were saying: 'You've got a big future at this club,

Ronnie. We believe in you and think you can make it to the top here and we are going to back you all the way. We are delighted with your progress and want to offer you an improved two-year contract, up from eight grand to ten. Well done.' A contract and pen were pushed across the desk towards me.

To be fair, their words may have been what they genuinely felt, but to me it sounded like the often repeated bullshit of a second-hand-car salesman.

I let them finish, then said, 'Thanks very much and I really appreciate the offer. It's been fantastic here. I've learned a lot and I love the county and its members, but it doesn't look as though I'm going to get an opportunity for some time. So I'm not sure I will be signing.'

They must have been expecting that because David Hughes said, 'I understand your feelings, Ronnie, but don't make a hasty decision. Take the contract with you and think about it.'

I picked it up and left the room, knowing the fact that they had offered me a new deal had reduced my chances of getting away. It meant I was a List One player. In order to stop a transfer market developing in cricket like there is in football, counties were only allowed to sign two List One players in five years, so the odds were slim that anyone would use up one of their vacancies on an untried rookie. I had to get my status changed to List Two, but to do that I needed to get the approval of the Lancashire committee. They had me by the balls and my chances of getting away were looking decidedly ropy. I was starting to think I might have to accept the contract, but a chance remark a few days later hardened my resolve to get away.

All the second-team players had arranged to meet in TGI

Friday in Sale for an end-of-season drink. It was a very emotional afternoon, very different from the many other occasions we'd been out as a group. Too many of the lads were suddenly out of work, their dreams shattered and their future uncertain. Those of us with contract offers felt embarrassed and unsure what to say. We had a few beers and a bit of banter but already it was no longer the same. It was uncomfortable and gradually two groups developed: those with contracts sat together and those who had been released seemed happier in another part of the bar where they could slag off the club and everyone connected with it.

I was sitting with Jason Gallian and John Crawley and they asked me what I was going to do.

'I don't really know. My instinct is to move. What do you think?'

Jason said, 'It's up to you, mate. But I guess it depends on how much you think they value you and if you believe they are going to give you the chance to achieve what you want.'

'Well, they've offered me a two-year deal and increased my money to ten grand, so I suppose they want me to stay.'

Jason and John looked at each other.

'What?' I asked.

Jason looked embarrassed. 'I don't know if this will help you, but we've both been offered twelve grand a year.'

I thought, Fucking bastards. They gave me all that crap in the meeting but didn't have the guts to say they didn't value me as much as my team-mates.

Jason started to apologise.

'No,' I said. 'Don't worry. It's not your fault. It's those bastards. But at least I know where I stand and what I have to do. Come on, I need another drink.'

Because I hadn't signed my contract, I got called in to see the chairman, Bob Bennett. He'd always been very straight with me and I hoped he would give me a sympathetic ear. England U19s happened to be playing at Old Trafford that day, so I went along a bit early in order to seek out Graham Saville and say hello. I hadn't seen him for a couple of years but I thought he might be able to give me some good advice. I found him in the gym next to the dressing rooms and we chatted away for a while, then he asked, 'What's going on here? You're a fantastic player but you're not getting a game. What are you going to do?'

I laughed. 'As a matter of fact, that's why I'm here. I've got a meeting with the chairman. I'm hoping to persuade him to make me a List Two player.

'Have you anything lined up?' he asked.

'Not really. I know Durham are interested and I've heard there might be a chance at Kent, Derbyshire or Glamorgan, and Yorkshire have put out feelers.'

'Let me know what happens,' he said. 'We'll have you at Essex.'

I could hardly believe my ears. Suddenly from having an uncertain future with lots of loose ends needing to be tied up, I had a whole new opportunity opening up at one of the top clubs in country – a club with a strong tradition and a long list of outstanding players such as Graham Gooch, Keith Fletcher, John Lever and further back to Doug Insole and Trevor Bailey.

'Really?' I asked.

'Sure. Keep in touch.'

Sav was a man I liked and admired and suddenly playing for Essex seemed like the best idea so far. Having walked into the gym feeling confused and unsure, I left thinking, Essex! I think I'll have a bit of that.

I went to meet Bob Bennett in the library, the same room where he had greeted me the day I signed.

'So, Ronnie, you are thinking of leaving us?'

I explained how I felt. I pointed out that Mike Watkinson had just been made captain and he was an all-rounder, so he was always going to be ahead of me, and that they already had other top all-rounders such as Wasim Akram and Phil de Freitas (I didn't know at the time that Phil was about to leave too). In addition, players such as Peter Martin and Glen Chapple were ahead of me, so I couldn't see a path to first-team cricket.

I added, 'Ian Austin is a good cricketer but he seldom gets a chance here. I'm coming up to 23 and I feel I need to get regular first-team cricket. I think I need to move on.'

The chairman nodded and said, 'I understand your position, but I'll be honest, I don't want you to go. I think you are a fine cricketer and you have a future here. Have you spoken to any other counties?'

I knew this was a tricky one because legally I wasn't yet free to talk to other clubs but Bob had always been straight with me and I decided to trust him. I told him I'd had a chat with a few people and knew that some counties were interested.

'Who are they?'

I told him. Again he nodded his head, as if to approve of what I was saying, so I decided to go the whole hog. 'And Essex have made me an offer,' I said, which wasn't a complete lie but was perhaps gilding the lily based on the conversation I'd had with Sav a few minutes before.

Bob's face changed. 'I've no problem with Durham or those other counties you mentioned,' he said. 'But I think it might be difficult if you chose Essex. People on the committee might object to that because we see them as one of our main competitors and you might strengthen them at our expense.'

I could hardly believe what I was hearing. It seemed it was OK for me to leave as long as I didn't go to a club where I might be successful and win things.

'Look,' Bob said. 'I'm very friendly with Keith Fletcher. I'll have a chat with him and see what we can sort out.'

Oh shit, I thought. Keith Fletcher doesn't know anything about it. I had to back down quickly and said, 'Don't bother, Bob. It probably won't come to anything anyway. I'm much more likely to go to Durham.'

We left it at that. He told me I had to write a letter to the committee, explaining why I wanted to leave and asking them to make me a List Two player. I went straight to see Rose Fitzgibbon who, together with Anne Murphy, ran the office at Lancashire. Rose was a gem, always friendly and helpful. She had been there when I signed, and whenever I'd been to her for anything it had never been any problem. She was a big cricket fan and a member of the committee. I explained that I had to compose this letter and asked her advice – letter-writing was one of the subjects I'd rather neglected at school – and she said, 'Don't worry, I'll draft it out for you to sign and I'll put your case to the committee. I don't want you to leave but I understand why you feel you must.'

True to her word, she did exactly as promised and a couple of weeks later I was told that I was a List Two player. Now I just had to sort out a contract with someone else.

CHAPTER 7

SOMEWHERE NEAR THE DARTFORD TUNNEL

It was time to get on the phone. I'd narrowed it down in my mind to Essex or Durham, and I needed to find out exactly what was on offer. Durham was quite an attractive proposition – they were only a couple of years into the county championship scene, had already attracted people like Ian Botham, Aussie David Boon, Johnny Morris, David Graveney, Paul Parker, Simon Hughes and Wayne Larkins, and I was reliably informed they were very keen to sign me. In addition, it was only a couple of hours away from home, which would be an advantage in view of my growing relationship with Lorraine and also getting back to see my parents. We all talked about it for hours, going over the pros and cons. The only thing I was certain of was that I desperately wanted to make it as a player and would do whatever it took to achieve that goal. Lorraine was brilliant, listening as I argued this way and that, and always said, 'Whatever you decide is best, I'll back you.'

I tried to get hold of Geoff Cook at Durham to find out what deal they had in mind. He wasn't an easy man to reach.

I spoke to his wife more than to him but eventually he told me they would pay me £18,000 a year and would try to get me a car and accommodation. There were a few bits and pieces I needed clarification on but each time I phoned it seemed that Geoff was in a meeting or away for a couple of days. I sensed he was after some bigger names and possibly juggling a budget. I guessed he didn't want to settle with me until he'd got his first targets in place and knew how much they would cost. I understood and respected that. I'd done nothing in the game so far and certainly wasn't the kind of star name who was going to put bums on seats at their matches.

The longer I agonised about it, the more I was leaning towards Essex. They were a big club and had won the county championship five times in the previous ten years. I liked the fact that they had a long tradition and wore old-fashioned jumpers with no colours, just the distinctive three-sabre badge. That was the kind of county I wanted to play for.

I rang John Bird, whose office is in Essex. The more I'd got to know him, the more I valued his advice and he said, 'Durham or Kent would be good for you, but I think you should play for Essex.'

'Why, John?'

'I employ people in every town in the country and the people of Essex are the nicest. They are genuine and warm, and if they have a problem with you they will stab you in the heart, not in the back. They have a lot of the best qualities of northerners but mixed with what's best about the south. I'm sure they will love the way you play cricket and will make you feel at home.'

I wanted to play cricket for people like that. As John Lennon said, 'A working-class hero is something to be.'

I needed to talk to Sav and make sure it was still on. As

usual, there was a snag – I'd forgotten to get his phone number and I could hardly ask at Old Trafford after my recent chat with the chairman. I remembered that John Crawley had been born in Malden in Essex before the family moved up to Lancashire. It was a long shot but worth a try. John's mother Jean had always been tremendous for me, taking her turn in driving John and me around to county representative matches, and his dad Frank was one of the guys you listened to when you were growing up because he always talked sense. I rang Jean and asked her if she'd got Sav's number. She hunted around for a bit, then came back and said, 'I haven't got a number but there's an address here. He lives in Great Notley, near Braintree. Try directory enquiries.'

There was no joy there, but, just as I was wondering what to do next, Jean phoned me back and said she'd managed to get hold of an office number for him. I thanked her for taking so much trouble and she said, 'Ronnie, we are sorry you are leaving Lancashire but you are a fine cricketer and we know you are going to make it wherever you go. Good luck.' It was just the encouragement I needed at that moment.

Jean died a few years before I retired and, although she was a different generation from me, it was like losing a friend. I felt so sad for John and gave him a big hug as we both bawled our eyes out. We were no longer as close as we'd been as teenagers but I knew what it must mean to him. At the crematorium, I looked across at my parents who were of a similar age to Jean. They had done so much for me. I cut the thoughts off. It was just too painful to think about.

When I called Sav's number, I got an answering machine, so I left a message asking him to call me. I heard nothing for two agonisingly long weeks. I didn't realise he was away on holiday and a million thoughts, most of them negative, kept going through my head while I waited for him to get back to me. I tried Geoff Cook again, but he was away. I was in limbo. Why hadn't I signed that Lancashire contract when they pushed it across the desk at me?

Finally, Sav rang me back. He'd had a word with the committee and he'd talked to Graham Gooch about me over a game of golf and they were happy to take his recommendation and sign me. He pointed out that there were no guarantees of a first-team place but, with Neil Foster and Derek Pringle recently retired, if I was half the cricketer he thought I was, I'd have a great chance of getting in the side. I assured him that was all I was asking for. It was all I'd ever asked for at Lancashire.

'There's a process to go through but it's on,' Sav said. 'What are you after money-wise?'

I wondered if I should mention that Durham had said they would pay me 18 grand but decided against it and just said, 'That's not my priority, Sav. I'm just happy to get the opportunity.'

A couple of days later, he came on again after a meeting with the club secretary Peter Edwards and said they were willing to pay me £12,000 a year and provide me with a car and a flat. It was six grand less than the Durham offer but Geoff had only said they would try to get the car and a flat. I hesitated for all of a second and said, 'Sav, that's great. I'm up for it. I want to play for Essex.'

What he didn't realise was that I was only vaguely aware of where Essex was. I knew it was down south and left a bit before you hit London and I remembered that it was somewhere near the Dartford Tunnel because after Nick Derbyshire and I played for England U17s at Chelmsford we set off in his car for a second ODI at Canterbury but broke down in the tunnel. I also had the feeling the sun always shone in Essex – or it had every time I'd played there. I recalled one four-day match with the second team on a great track. Ian Folley was in one of his 'fuck Lancashire' moods and, when he was sent in as night watchman, he heaved two massive sixes before squandering his wicket the following ball. We'd found some great bars that trip and I seem to recall that the team got quite hammered one night.

I'd also been to Ilford as twelfth man for the first team – a terrible job that means you are basically a gofer who carries the drinks and does jobs around the dressing room. But during the game some of the Essex fans had come up to me and said they remembered me playing in the England U19s, which was nice. I liked the way the local crowd applauded good cricket, whichever side played it. I'd also had a good time in the evening around Romford and even sorted the lads out a table at the dog track courtesy of Coral. Essex may have been something of a dark continent to me, but the little I knew was positive.

The other thing that Sav didn't realise when he made the offer was that I'd been struggling for a few months with a groin injury that had spread to my hip towards the end of the season. I was in agony in the last few matches – it was as though someone was thrusting a knife into my hip joint – but I was young and could play through the pain without too much difficulty. Now I had a dilemma. I needed to get it fixed but I also wanted to get away for the winter and play some cricket so that I was in good form ready for my new challenge. I decided I'd try to do both at the same time.

Jack Simmons asked me to go up to Bowlers, his indoor cricket centre in Manchester, and said he'd been asked to recommend someone to play in New Zealand that winter and, if I wanted it, the job was mine. 'There's no real money in it,' he said, 'but they'll pay your air fare, provide you with a place to stay and a car. The guy over there is Paul Lucas. I don't know him but judging by his letters he seems a good bloke. He'll give you some work and pay your expenses to do some kids' coaching.'

I said I'd love to take it and thanked Jack for thinking of me.

He shook my hand and said, 'I don't want you to leave Old Trafford – you've got steel and you're a good cricketer. However – and I shouldn't say this because I'm on the committee – I think you are doing the right thing. Essex is a tip-top county and you'll do well there.' Jack was a proper Lancastrian, honest as the day is long.

Within a couple of weeks, I was on my way to New Zealand. I'd drawn out all my £1,500 savings which got me around 4,000 New Zealand dollars and I planned to use it to sort out my injury problems. I was determined to make the most of the next few months to get myself in great nick before heading to Essex.

Jack's gut feeling about Paul Lucas was spot on. He's a successful businessman with a lovely family. They live in Epsom, just outside the city of Auckland and he and his wife Tina invited me to stay with them. They had a daughter, Kate, who was at school, and two sons, Matt and Daniel, who were away at university. The family took me under their wing and I quickly settled into a home from home.

Also on the trip with me was Joe Grant, a strapping West Indian fast bowler, who had played a bit for Jamaica and was later to join me at Essex after a stint in the Lancashire leagues. Joe's a powerful man with a big heart and he and I enjoyed each other's company. We had a great time coaching the youngsters who were keen to learn. Joe's only problem was that he had a short fuse and if he thought people were being awkward or racist he would let them have it. A West Indian face was quite a rarity in those parts so there were a few dodgy moments, such as the time we were out in town and a family stopped in their tracks and stared at Joe as though he had two heads. 'What are you looking at?' he snapped and started towards them. They high-tailed it out of there and I grabbed Joe and told him to forget it. 'You've got to ignore people like that,' I said. 'You'll only get yourself into trouble.' He clearly wasn't convinced and the next time we had hassle it wasn't so easy to hold him back. And, if anything, I was ready to join him.

It happened when we drove into a ground where we were due to play that afternoon and Joe parked in a spot near the pavilion. We started to get our gear out of the boot when a guy came over and shouted, 'Hey, blackie, you can't park there.'

I saw Joe pick up a stump from his bag and just managed to grab his arm. Keeping him behind me, I said to the guy, 'You are bang out of order. That's just plain racist.'

'Well, he can't park there.'

'Why? Because he's black?'

'That spot is for special people.'

Joe was still behind me and I could feel that he was about to explode. 'Look, pal,' I said, 'we're playing here this afternoon. Is that special enough for you? Now I suggest, if you want to stay healthy, you get out of my face and stay out of it for the rest of the day, otherwise you'll have two of us to deal with.'

The guy slunk away.

I said to Joe, 'I know you'd like to kill him but, trust me,

I've been there. He isn't worth it. Wankers like that will get nowhere in life.'

Joe gave me a half-smile. 'Yeah, I trust you, Tiger. But it riles me. Now let's go and take it out on some batsman.'

The standard of cricket was good and I scored runs and took wickets, but my groin and hip were hurting badly and after about six weeks my knee blew up. I knew I had to get it fixed – I dared not go to Essex injured – and after making enquiries I went to see Dr Tony Edwards, a young orthopaedic surgeon in St Helier Bay.

The first difference I noticed was that there was no rigmarole about needing to be referred by a GP. I just walked into his reception and booked an appointment. He took a look at me, put me on a course of anti-inflammatories and referred me to Graeme White for physiotherapy. After three weeks I was still struggling so I went back. Tony examined my swollen knee, then stuck a needle in it and drained off about 90mls of fluid. As soon as he did it, the knee felt good. It was as though all the pressure had been eased. He also had the results of an MRI scan he'd done and said, 'You've got a lot of scar tissue in the knee. What have you had done?'

'I had a cyst removed from behind the knee when I was about 17.'

'Looks to me as though they didn't know what they were doing. But don't worry, we can get you right.'

I felt he was someone I could trust. I emphasised how important it was that I sorted out all my problems before I went home, and he said that, while he couldn't fix the hip and groin trouble, he knew someone who could. He arranged for Stewart Walsh, another young orthopaedic consultant, to examine me and he explained that the two lots of pain were connected. 'If we sort out the hip, we'll sort out the groin,' he said. 'You've just got some inflammation in the joint and, if I can drop some cortisone on it, that should do the trick. You'll feel great as soon as it's done but you mustn't train or play cricket for three weeks afterwards.'

I was concerned that the club would send me home if I was out of action that long but, when I spoke to Paul, he said it wasn't a problem because there was a long break over the Christmas period so I could fit in the treatment then.

For Stewart to inject the joint, I had to lie on my back with my knees raised and legs splayed out like a woman giving birth. He then slid a needle in through the groin area and into the hip. It didn't reach at first so he fitted a longer needle and this time I let out a yelp of pain. 'That's the spot,' he said and dropped the cortisone right on it. The only way I can explain the impact is to say it was like those Gaviscon TV adverts for heartburn where the firemen are in the stomach spraying soothing liquid to cool things down. What a feeling, indeed. I knew in an instant that he'd done the trick. He circled my leg around and there was absolutely no pain. He took me outside and made me sprint a couple of shuttles and again I didn't feel a thing.

'Make sure you rest it up for three weeks and you should be fine,' he said. I could have hugged him.

Sure enough, three weeks later, I was able to train hard and play without a problem. I was just over £1,000 poorer but I felt great. It was an enormous relief and a good lesson. I swore from that day on I was going to take charge of looking after my body and always seek out the best advice even if it cost me.

A good chunk of the rest of my cash went on a podiatrist that Tony Edwards introduced me to. I'd been wearing insoles since I was a kid to help with shin-splint and knee problems but this guy was something else. He recommended that I switched to Asics shoes. They didn't do a cricket shoe, so we adapted a cross-trainer by taking the sole off and adding spikes. He also took a cast of my foot and made me my first customised insoles. The difference was incredible. For several years, I spent hundreds of pounds having special insoles flown in from New Zealand but it was worth every penny.

I enjoyed my last few weeks over there, playing cavalier, painless cricket. I felt sharp. I was seeing the ball well, scoring runs and taking wickets. I thanked the Lucas family for their hospitality and headed back to England, eager to start my new life.

CHAPTER 8
LOSTOCK TO CHELMSFORD – THE LONGEST JOURNEY

Dad smiled to break the tension. 'Don't worry. I can always get you a job as a butcher if it doesn't work out.' I'd only been home a few days after three months in New Zealand but now I was off again. Dad said goodbye before he went to bed. He left for work every day at six o'clock so wouldn't see me in the morning. 'Ronnie, I just want to wish you luck. My only advice is to play so well that they find it impossible to leave you out of the team. I know you can do it. And remember, we are always here for you.'

As I gave him a hug, it dawned on me that I was leaving home for good. This would be the last time I would sleep in that room overlooking Heaton cricket ground as a resident of that house. More than ever before I was hit by the enormity of what I was doing. I was leaving a whole part of my life behind me for good and stepping off the high board without even knowing how deep the water was below me.

At least, I thought, Lorraine will be near. Over the last few years she'd been studying to become a nursery nurse and had written to me in New Zealand to tell me she too had got a job down south so we could still see each other regularly. The only snag was that her geography was no better than mine. She'd taken a job in Aylesbury and we soon discovered we were still a good couple of hours apart.

The next morning, Mum cooked my breakfast and prepared to drive me to the station. We were both close to tears, so the conversation was a bit stilted, saying irrelevant things but not daring to say what we felt. I wore my blazer to travel in and had four bags – two with my bats, pads, gloves, size-12 boots and the rest of my cricket gear, the other two with the rest of my life in. Mum dropped me off at Lostock railway station at the start of one of the saddest yet most exciting journeys of my life. I kissed her goodbye, determined that I would make her and Dad proud of me and reward them for all the effort and love they had put into getting me to this important point of my life.

As a kid I'd twice been to India with the Bolton touring teams Dad had organised. More recently I'd been to South Africa with Nick Derbyshire, to Australia with England U19s and that winter to New Zealand. But this journey to Essex was by far the most daunting I'd undertaken.

I heaved one bag over each shoulder, picked up another in each hand and lugged them on to the train from Lostock to Bolton, from there to Manchester Victoria and then finally to Manchester Piccadilly, where I bought a one-way ticket to London. Normally, it's a straightforward run into Euston, taking a couple of hours or so, but there had been a derailment and they announced we were being diverted via Sheffield and Nottingham. What they didn't tell us was that we were no longer heading for Euston and the trip would now take more than four hours.

It was probably the longest four hours of my life, a real

stomach-churning journey during which I experienced every emotion imaginable. I felt very alone. I was the only son and I knew my parents would have preferred me to be closer to home. It may seem an odd thing to say these days, but back then Essex was a long way from Bolton and most people didn't just jump in the car and drive a couple of hundred miles or so as they do today.

But I also felt angry and defiant. The system at Lancashire had never given me the chance to fulfil my potential and that had forced me to take this giant step. I knew I had given my all while I was there but they had never rewarded my effort.

I was also a little nervous about the kind of reception I was likely to get when pre season training started the following day. I'd met some of the Essex guys from playing with them in England teams and against them in the second XI, but it still felt a bit like the first day at a new school, wondering how the southerners would take to a gobby lad from Bolton. But I'd learned a lot from Fil about mixing with people and getting on with strangers, so I was reasonably confident I could carry it off, especially as my other emotion right then was elation.

In short, I was pleased that I'd taken my courage in both hands and made the decision to leave Old Trafford. It would have been easier to stay and hope for the best but I felt that would have been letting down both me and my dreams. I was proud that I had taken control of my destiny and I was excited at what lay ahead.

As the train meandered slowly down the centre of England, all these emotions swirled around in my head. I stared blankly out the window, lost in a million contrasting thoughts, barely noticing anything we passed. As the time dragged by, I became anxious about being late on my first day and cursed the train that had chosen this of all days to go off the rails. But through all this turmoil I kept coming back to a central belief: this is my big chance. I want to be a successful cricketer. I am going to be a successful cricketer. I'll show them at Old Trafford. I'll make Lorraine, my family and friends proud of me. I will make this work. I have to make this work.

Graham Saville had told me to make my way to the ground at Chelmsford, where someone would meet me and take me to my new flat. With no mobile phones back then, I was unable to let them know why I was late, so, as soon as the train pulled into the station, I ran through the ticket barrier and found a phone box. With 6ft 4in of me and four large bags it was a bit crowded in there and I had to fumble around for some change. Eventually, I got through and a voice the other end said, 'Essex County Cricket Club, Malcolm Field speaking.'

'Hi, Malcolm, my name is Ronnie Irani. I'm just joining Essex but my train has been held up because of a derailment.' I was aware that I was gabbling because I was so keen to let them know it wasn't my fault I was late.

Malcolm, who was the assistant to secretary Peter Edwards, was calm at the other end. And he sounded really welcoming. 'Ronnie, good to hear from you. We are expecting you. There's no problem – just make your way to Chelmsford. Paul Prichard's going to take you to your flat. Where are you now?'

I didn't have a clue. I looked around me, spotted the sign and said, 'I'm at St Pancreas station.'

I heard a laugh at the other end of the phone. 'I think you'll find that's St Pancras, Ronnie. Pancreas is your stomach. Just take the tube to Liverpool Street and you can get a train from there. See you soon.'

I heaved my bags back into place and made my way on to the underground, trying not to wipe out too many commuters as I went. Eventually I got to Liverpool Street, found platform 12 and clambered aboard the Chelmsford train. At the other end I decided to splash out on a taxi to the county ground. A minute and a half later, the cab stopped and the driver said with a smile, 'Here you are, mate. Essex County Cricket Club.'

'Sorry,' I stammered, 'I didn't realise it was so close.'

'No problem, mate. There's a minimum fare so you've done me a favour.'

As I made my way towards the pavilion, I saw George Clarke, the dressing-room attendant. He was a lovely old boy and I'd chatted to him a few times when I'd played there but I didn't think he would remember me. He came over as soon as he saw me, shook my hand and said, 'Ronnie, good to see you again. I'm so pleased you've joined Essex. I can't believe Lancashire let you go but their loss is our gain.'

After more than five hours travelling, the hassle, the doubts and the sheer bloody loneliness of not knowing what was in store for me, those few words were just what I needed. For the first time in years, I felt I was at a club that wanted me. George's warmth has always stuck with me: it meant so much I even mentioned it in my wedding speech.

As promised, Paul Prichard was there to meet me and he too played an important part in making me feel welcome. He drove me to his home to have something to eat with his family before taking me on to my new flat in Colchester. It wasn't a big welcome do or anything like that, just a very pleasant family meal and a thoughtful gesture.

If I hadn't been greeted so warmly, I might well have turned round and gone home when I saw the flat I was to share with

Richard Pearson, a young off-spinner from Yorkshire and a former England U19 team-mate who was also joining the ground staff. It was on the ground floor, dark, not particularly well furnished or decorated, and had carpets that had seen better days. It had a small living room, kitchen, shower, two bedrooms and an odd smell, like rotting fish. It took me two weeks to track down that stink. I looked behind cupboards, in dark nooks and crannies, went all over the flat sniffing like a bloodhound until finally I realised it was coming from an old light fitting that stank as it warmed up. I'm not sure what that said about the wiring but at least the smell went away when we put in a new fitting.

Having just got back from living in luxury with the Lucas family, and having left the home comforts that included Mum doing my washing and ironing, this was a bit of a comedown. There was no Sky TV so I had to rely on 5 live to hear my beloved Manchester United make another title charge. But the welcome I'd received made me optimistic. I soon discovered there was a laundrette just up the road with an inexpensive service wash and a superb Chinese takeaway opposite. Fuck it, I thought. This will do just fine. Get on with it, Ronnie. You've got people to impress.

CHAPTER 9

ARE YOU WATCHING, LANCASHIRE?

George, our dressing room attendant, was also a qualified umpire and he took charge of our pre-season inter-squad matches. Having regained full fitness and form in New Zealand, I was already firing on all cylinders and relished the chance to show what I could do, especially against Graham Gooch. This was my chance to impress the captain – and my new team-mates. I steamed in and let go a beauty that smacked against Goochie's pad. I roared my appeal and, to my delight, George's finger went up. I was enjoying my cricket more than I had for years.

The first rule of entering a new dressing room is that silence is golden. Listen more than you talk and choose your moments to make an impact. I'd gained a reputation around Old Trafford as being a bit brash and never shy to give my opinion. I also enjoyed the banter and could give as well as take, but I was determined not to get on the wrong side of anyone early on at Essex and turned most of my jokes against myself.

In all honesty, settling in wasn't a problem. It was made

easier because it was John Childs's benefit year so I got to hang out with the lads socially and met a number of the members and supporters at his events. The fans seemed pleased to have the chance to quiz the new boy about what he hoped to achieve with the county, while the players appreciated that I was willing to do my bit to support John. It all helped me be accepted. But really it was no great effort on my part. I had nothing much to fill the time when I wasn't training and, having grown up around the local cricket clubs at home, I was used to these occasions and enjoyed them.

The Essex dressing room was very friendly anyway, taking their lead from Graham Gooch, a legend as a cricketer, much funnier than his public image suggests and just a great bloke to be around. He was 41 years old by this time but still one of the keenest trainers, setting a great example from the front. And he had everyone's respect as a player. Although he'd handed over the England captaincy, he was still first pick as his country's opening bat. It crossed my mind that the England lads would be noticing a difference between Graham's style and the more aloof, autocratic way Mike Atherton went about his job.

At that stage Keith Fletcher was manager of England but he was still a big influence around the place. I once read an article that credited Fletch with making Essex 'the happiest and most successful of the 18 first-class counties' and I wouldn't argue with that. I got to know him even better when he returned to his beloved Essex as our coach the following year. He only set one goal – to try to win every game. He was brilliant at man-management. He wasn't a rabble-rouser; he preferred to have a quiet word with individuals, but what he said always made a lot of sense. He made you feel good about yourself and your ability and, what's more, he introduced me to fly-fishing at East Hanningfield reservoir for which I'm eternally grateful.

As well as a good dressing room, Chelmsford had one other advantage over Old Trafford – the temperature was two or three degrees warmer than in Manchester and it didn't rain nearly as much, making pre-season training in March a more pleasant experience. There was a serious side to that because, while it was nice to have your pre-season in South Africa or the West Indies, we could train outside at home and spend plenty of time in the nets in the kind of conditions we would face when the season started.

As a junior member of the squad, you don't get much batting time early on but I did a lot of bowling shifts and put in a bit of extra effort when facing Graham Gooch. I even lifted the seam a bit to get some extra movement and the skipper would nod and say, 'Good ball.' I smacked a few runs in the inter-squad matches and did well in a second-team match, taking four wickets up at Cambridge.

I was wondering if I'd done enough to make the team when Lady Luck decided to give me a leg up. Essex had signed my old Australian U19 adversary Michael Kasprowicz to boost their pace attack. In training he bowled one that flew up and hit John Stephenson on the hand, breaking his finger. As an England all-rounder and a senior member of the Essex squad, John was probably the man who would keep me out of the side. Suddenly he wasn't able to play and the season was just around the corner. Essex decided to take a chance. They threw me into the first game, against Hampshire at the old Southampton ground, a place I'd played before and liked. I bowled OK, got a few runs, we won the match and I kept my place. I was on my way.

My new county was turning out to be everything I could have hoped for. Richard and I had even managed to brighten up the flat a bit and make it more comfortable. The only thing that hadn't materialised yet was the car I'd been promised. Paul Prichard was still driving us in every day but I was keen to get some wheels of my own. Getting a sponsored car was a big deal for a young pro. You couldn't afford to buy anything decent and I thought Essex's connections with Ford might see me in line for a nice little run-around, but each time I approached the marketing manager, Kit Brockley, he fobbed me off with the sponsored-car version of 'the cheque's in the post'.

Finally, he told me he'd got something sorted out. I arranged with Graham Gooch to have the afternoon off and made my way to Kit's office, still wearing my tracksuit trousers with grass stains on the knees and a rip in one leg where I'd tried to pull them over my cricket boots. I did have a clean T-shirt on but it would have looked much smarter if I'd mastered the art of ironing.

'What car is it?' I asked as nonchalantly as I could muster.

'We're not quite sure yet,' Kit said.

That seemed an odd answer as we were just about to pick it up. Oh hell, I thought, they've got me a Lada and don't want to tell me. How can I go back to Old Trafford in that?

'Sorry to be vague,' Kit said, 'but it's a company we haven't dealt with before. It's a new name to us and we're not sure what it is. But don't worry, I'm certain it will be OK and, if it's not, we'll arrange something else in a few weeks.'

I was more convinced than ever that it was a Lada and that he'd decided that, whatever it was, it would be good enough for a junior player, newly on the staff. I made up my mind that whatever happened I would just be grateful for having something to get me around. I could always hitch a lift with someone else when we played Lancashire.

We set off in Kit's car, which I noticed was a rather nice Volvo, and headed for Dukes Park industrial estate near Chelmsford. Kit wasn't sure exactly where he was going, but after consulting his directions he turned into a forecourt of a Jaguar main dealer. 'This must be it,' he said, sounding very unsure.

It was impossible not to be extremely impressed when we stepped in to this immaculate, chrome and glass reception area. In fact, I felt a bit self-conscious because I was looking so scruffy. Kit introduced himself and the woman behind the desk said, 'Oh yes, they are expecting you in the board room,' and ushered us upstairs into this swish room, where we met MD Mike Flannery and a couple of the other directors. I looked round for the hidden cameras convinced this was an elaborate initiation wind-up that was being videoed to show my new team-mates.

Mike, a Scotsman, greeted us warmly and offered us coffee. Then he made a little speech: 'Ronnie, we are delighted to welcome you to Essex and hope you are going to have a long and successful stay with the club. We've found out a bit about you and are delighted to be associated with you. We want you to know that, if there's ever anything we can do to help, just give us a call. You are a new, exciting, young player so we think it is appropriate that you should be associated with a new, exciting, young car. Not many people have heard of this model yet but we firmly believe it's going to be one of the leading cars on the road. It's a two-litre turbo and has great speed and agility – a real wolf in sheep's clothing.'

I was still sure this was a wind-up, although I noticed that, behind a rather fixed smile, Kit's face had turned grey. I said a few words of thanks and, after a bit more general chat, we were led back downstairs where the showroom manager was sent to fetch the car. I looked out the window, expecting something like Del Trotter's Reliant Robin van to appear, driven by some of the Essex lads. But when the car reversed towards me all I noticed was it had two exhausts! I didn't dare believe it was mine. But there it was in all its glory – a white Subaru Legacy Turbo. I had just been handed the best car on the Essex staff.

'There you are, Ronnie,' Kit murmured. 'I told you we would take care of you.' But I could sense he was cursing himself, knowing he was going to get so much stick from senior players. He'd obviously thought Subaru was another Lada and had not bothered to check. He'd fucked up big time but that was not my problem. This little baby had 'Ronnie Irani, Essex CCC' inscribed along the side and it was all mine.

'Thanks, Kit,' I said trying not to gloat, but unable to suppress a huge grin. 'You're a top man.'

I climbed inside. It had every gadget you could wish for and that fantastic 'fresh from the showroom' smell. I touched the throttle and the beast roared at me. I said my farewells and eased it gently into the road. I hit the accelerator and it took off like a jet plane. I flicked the switch to open my window, punched the air and yelled at the top of my voice, 'You fucking beauty!' I couldn't wait for the day when I could turn into Old Trafford and park next to the rather less stylish motors of my former team-mates.

There are people who reckon you shouldn't give young players too much too early because they get into a comfort zone and think they've made it. That might be true for some people but believe me that car I'd got with a two-year sponsorship deal just made me even more determined to do well. I had to live up to it. And it also made me think that, if I really got my act together, there could be plenty of other rewards out there.

The lads gave me quite a lot of good-natured stick about my new motor – but not nearly as much as they gave Kit. However, it also triggered a couple of incidents that made me wonder about Nasser Hussain. He was a few years older than me, had been in the Essex side for a number of years and was already an England player. He had been friendly enough when I arrived but I had noticed that he was a bit of a loner and could be quite sharp and aggressive with his team-mates at times. He was definitely one of the senior players and I quickly decided that it would be sensible to get on with him. I didn't think anything of it when he asked to take the Subaru for a spin. He had a big Peugeot that his dad sponsored and I presume it must have been quite a solid motor because when he climbed into mine he hammered it. He revved it like hell and two weeks later I had to take it back to get a new clutch fitted.

I was a bit upset but didn't say anything. However, not long after, I decided it was time for me to stand up to him and make my mark over another incident. I had always been taught to be polite, and every birthday and Christmas Mum and Dad wouldn't allow me to play with my new toys until I'd sat down and written the thank-you letters. It was a chore because, as I've said, letter-writing doesn't come easy to me, but by now it was second nature and one afternoon I got some Essex letterhead paper and started to write to Mike Flannery to thank him for sponsoring me. I was in the dressing room, kneeling on the floor with the paper on the bench. I took great care, composing exactly what I wanted to say and writing carefully so it looked good. It took me at least 40 minutes. As I was finishing up, Nasser came in off the balcony and went through to the toilet, making a couple of cracks about what a sad bastard I was to be writing letters to my sponsors. As he came back through, the breeze from the door blew the letter on to the floor and, before I could retrieve it, he stepped straight on it with his spikes.

It looked deliberate to me and I was livid. 'Hey! You fucking twat. What the hell do you think you are doing?'

He looked a bit startled that I'd fronted him up. 'What's up? It's only a letter,' he said and walked back out on the balcony where a few other players were standing chatting.

I followed him out and had a right go at him. I told him that if he ever did anything like that again I would rip his face open. The rest of the balcony went very quiet. This was a side of me they hadn't seen. I went and got another sheet of paper and rewrote the letter, wondering if there would be any repercussions but overall I thought it was probably a good thing that I'd stood up for myself. Even in a good dressing room like Essex, people need to know you can't be put upon.

It certainly seemed to do the trick with Nasser because I was seldom on the wrong end of his tongue after that. In fact, over the next few years we would often drive to matches together. He was always quiet, but I could talk for two and, if he was driving, I'd often catch up on my sleep. It developed into a kind of friendship. We spent a lot of time in each other's company, yet I never felt that we got really close. He wasn't very sociable – if the lads invited him out, he'd usually say, 'I spend all day with you lot – why would I want to see you in the evenings?' And when he was made England

Above left: My mother Anne helps me cut the cake on my first birthday.

Above right: Outside our back door aged five at Heaton Cricket Club – I only had to jump over the fence to play.

Below left: When I was four Mum took me on a daytrip to Blackpool – only 39 miles from Bolton.

Below right: Aged five-and-a-half, getting some useful batting tips from an 18-year-old Javed Miandad, who played professionally at Dad's Daisy Hill Club.

Above: In the back garden at Atherton with my friend Gillian, ready to receive a few deliveries from Dad.

Middle: Almost five years old and holding the trophy with my dad Jimmy and Javed, after Daisy Hill won the league championship for the third time on the trot.

Below right: A grainy shot of me in the front room, of course, with a cricket bat.

Above left: My dad played local league cricket for 40-odd years and I was on the pitch before I could even walk.

Above right: Popular with the ladies on my fifth birthday.

Middle: Ex-Lancashire and India wicket-keeper/batsman Farokh Engineer gave me many great tips. You can see a few of my cricket and football trophies in the background.

Below left: At a very early age, somewhere between eight and ten, with the season's collection of trophies and individual prizes for cricket.

Above: Lorraine and I on our wedding day.

Below left: As a Heaton pro in July 1990.
The Bolton News

Below right: Athletics coach Frank Dick, one of my mentors.

Above left: Wasim Akram was the man who introduced me to the magic of reverse swing.

Photo by Richard Rollon, Bolton Evening News, December 05 1991.

Above right: Graham Gooch and I scored many runs together and caught a few fish.

Below: Fil Adams and I pose for a publicity shot for our fruit and veg shop.

The Bolton News

Above: My mentor John Bird in the executive suite at Chelmsford, watching me score a century.

Right: Celebrating my first Test wicket, Mohammad Azharuddin caught by Nick Knight at Edgbaston on 6 June 1996.

Left: Two of the men who played a huge part in my career, Graham Saville and Keith Fletcher.

Below: The England lads congratulate me after I dismiss India's Ajay Jadeja at Lord's in June 1996.

Above: Whyte & Mackay awards winners in September 1996. I was Best All-Rounder, Graham Gooch was Best Batsman and Alec Stewart was Cricketer of the Year.

Below: What a feeling. The Essex lads celebrate winning the Totesport National League in 2006.

© *Kieran Galvin*

captain that became the only thing he cared about. He reminded me a lot of Mike Atherton in that way.

Those two incidents apart, I couldn't have asked for a better start to my life in Essex. I hit a half-century in my second match against Durham and took a career-best 4-27 against Kent in the following game. Before the end of May, I had beaten my best ever first-class score with 83 against the New Zealand tourists. It was going like a dream for me and, every time I had a good day, I thought about the people back in Lancashire. I knew Mum and Dad would be thrilled and relieved. There would be a number of supporters who would see what I was doing and say, 'I told you we shouldn't have let him go.' And I imagined some people in the Lancashire dressing room watching the scores tick over on Ceefax and cursing. It made my success even more satisfying.

The icing on the cake came early in June when I hit my maiden first-class century with Graham Gooch at the other end. We went to Worcestershire unbeaten in our opening five matches and with three wins under our belt. It was a terrific track for batsmen but even so I managed to pick up four wickets in their first innings as they piled on 381. We were bowled out well short of that, despite a century from Goochie and 50 from me. Then, with Graeme Hick and Tom Moody whacking it wherever they wanted, Worcester declared, leaving us to make 405 in a day to win. That certainly didn't look on when Nasser was caught by Gavin Haynes for a duck at 133-3. But Graham was in imperious form and I felt good, and we set about chasing the runs. We put on 245 in double-quick time.

As well as the joy of scoring my first century, it was an education to watch Gooch at his best. He scored 205, his third double-century of the season and his third hundred in a row. It was the first time I'd been at the other crease with a batsman playing the reverse sweep. That was impressive enough but then, when a short ball came down, he got down on one knee and improvised a shot I'd never seen anywhere before. Then he walked down the pitch, prodded it with his bat and said in that slightly high-pitched voice of his, 'Reverse pull. If you pay attention, I'll teach you that one day.'

I was totally in awe of the man. I had to leap out of the way when he rocketed a straight drive past me to the boundary and again he strolled up the pitch to share the moment: 'Probably my favourite shot. It shows the bowler you are in control. Straight back past him before he can get down and stop it. Have a bit of that!'

I was getting a masterclass from one of the finest batsmen this country has ever produced. When he was in that form, the bowlers just didn't know where to bowl and the captain couldn't set a field to stop him. We went on to win the game by four wickets off the last ball and took over at the top of the county championship table. Days don't get much better than that.

CHAPTER 10
A YOUNG THRUSTER

If batting with one of my heroes had made my first century memorable, the second sticks in the mind for a very different reason. I've always thought there was something odd about men's urinals – a row of guys with their dicks in their hands, staring fixedly at a blank wall to convince themselves they have some privacy. So I guess it should be no surprise that one of the most bizarre moments of my life happened in a public toilet.

We were playing Middlesex at Uxbridge, one of their out grounds. It's different from most county grounds in that the public come and go freely through the pavilion. At the end of the first day's play, most of the lads went to the bar for a beer but Michael Kasprowicz wanted to bowl in the nets and I agreed to bat against him. I was next in the following morning and, with John Stephenson on his way back to fitness, I was happy to get as much practice as I could to keep hold of my place in the side. We had a good session, and afterwards, as Kasper went to get the dressing-room key, I popped into the toilet, which was part of the shower and locker room area. I was still padded up and wearing spikes so I walked rather tentatively on the tiled floor, knowing it would be easy to end up in a heap on the deck.

I was making my way towards the urinals a bit like Bambi on ice when a guy shoved past me. I didn't say anything and started to pee. But then he looked down the row and, for no reason I could tell, gave me a right gobful of abuse. Or I think it was abuse. His face was certainly screwed up as though he hated my guts but he was so drunk it was hard to make out what he was saying.

As well as teaching you to walk away from trouble whenever you can, martial arts training also gives you the confidence to handle dodgy situations. You know that if you are sober you have a much better than even chance of tackling a drunk, so I smiled and said nothing. He was still gobbing off and finally, as I zipped myself up, I said, 'Sorry, pal, I can't make out what you're saying. What's your problem?'

What happened next takes longer to describe than it did in real time. He slung a huge haymaker at me. I only saw it at the last minute and, as I turned away, my spikes slipped on the tiles. His fist whacked straight into my eye. My contact lens shot out and as it fell I stuck out a hand and caught it. At the same time I was desperately trying to keep my balance and wondering what the hell was going on.

The effort of throwing the punch put matey off balance and he went careering across the room and knocked over a tray of pint glasses left in the other side of the changing room. As I heard them smash, I thought, Oh, shit. I was off balance with one good eye, one hand clutching my contact lens and a drunken bastard was possibly about to come at me with broken glass. I'd once seen the effect of a glassing back in Bolton that had resulted in a lost eye. I had to get out of there fast.

Fortunately, at that moment Kasper came in. He's even bigger than me and he managed to grab the drunk and bundle him out. I made my way to the dressing room, slipped my lens in my toilet bag, put on my trainers and thought, Right, I'm going to have that bastard. By the time I got outside, he was about 40 yards away being escorted towards the exit by stewards. I went after him, but some of the lads had heard what had happened and caught up with me. I heard Goochie say, 'Leave it, Ronnie. Let the stewards handle it.'

I knew he was right. There were several people about and, if I'd thumped him, it would have become a big story with me in the wrong. I went over to the guy, put my face close to his and said, 'What the fuck was all that about? Look what you've done to my eye.'

He looked bemused, as though he'd never seen me before. He just slurred 'Whaat?' and staggered off. Every muscle in my body longed to give him a thrashing but I turned away.

I went for an x-ray and fortunately the cheekbone wasn't broken, but I spent the rest of the evening icing away the bruising and spitting blood. When I woke the next morning, I couldn't see out of the eye and had to start icing it again. It hurt like hell but I was determined I was going to bat. My eye was still sore when I went to the crease and there was no disguising the big black bruise. Being the gentleman he is, Phil Tufnell kept bowling the ball up high, forcing me to squint into the sun. There was nothing much I could do except kick them away but eventually I adjusted, started to pick them up and went on to score a hundred.

The drunk received a caution from the police and wrote me a letter saying how sorry he was. I rang him up and he was full of apologies. He swore he would never do anything like that again and I said, 'Well, at least you were big and brave enough to admit you were wrong. Not everyone would have done that.'

Generally, life at Essex was good. I particularly enjoyed a half-century against Lancashire when I had to concentrate hard on a Chelmsford pitch that for once gave the seamers plenty of help. It was only July and I'd already played more games for Essex than I had in all my years at Old Trafford. Effort and form counted for something at Chelmsford in a way they hadn't at Lancashire. My first trip back to Old Trafford didn't come until the following season. It felt a bit strange, not at all like 'going home'. There were still many of the familiar faces I felt had not given me a chance and even my former second-team-mates were now determined I wouldn't shine on the day. Warren Hegg was the only person who went out of his way to make me welcome. But things were very different when I went out to bat. The members and crowd gave me a terrific reception all the way to the crease and I was relieved that they at least understood how much I had wanted to play for Lancashire and why I had to leave.

I was also settling in well domestically in Essex. After a period of driving to and from Aylesbury, I'd finally persuaded Lorraine that we'd be better able to save to get married if I wasn't spending a fortune on petrol. Of course, my motives had nothing to do with a dislike of ironing or, perish the thought, lustful intentions, I was just doing what I could to hasten the day when I could afford to make an honest woman of her. Incredibly, she agreed to move in with me.

I finished off the 1994 season in good nick. I'd played 18 county championship matches and scored just under a thousand runs at an average of almost 42 and taken 28 wickets costing less than 30 each. I had a relaxing winter and looked forward to my second season at my new home.

This was the period when I should have kicked on, especially with my bowling, but I started to get a nagging pain in my back. I had some physio which partly eased the problem, but I knew I'd lost a bit of pace and was stiffening up after a day's play and finding it harder to warm up in the morning. I didn't realise it at the time but I'd picked up a stress fracture in my back. I carried on playing through the pain and did well enough, compensating for the slight loss of pace with more accuracy, enthusiasm and bloody-minded determination. But, looking back, this was a key period and, if I'd sorted it out then, it would have saved me a lot of problems later.

We had a new captain at Essex in 1995. Graham Gooch had stepped down, although he carried on playing for another couple of seasons, and Paul Prichard took up the reins. While I was disappointed not to have another season under Graham, I'd come to realise that Prich was Essex through and through and I had no problem about him taking over. One or two people at the club weren't as sure because he liked to have a drink and a laugh after a day's play, and I know that Nasser was among those who felt he wouldn't be a good influence on the younger players. Whatever the rights and wrongs of it, Prich can boast that we won two Lord's finals while he was in charge.

My averages weren't quite so good in my second season but I'd still done well and people in the national media were beginning to take notice of me. It was particularly pleasing to pick up the *Daily Mirror* towards the end of the campaign and read Ian Botham's column, in which he urged the England selectors to take an all-rounder on the winter tour to South Africa, adding, 'Let's give Ronnie Irani, the best young all-rounder in the country, a chance at the top level.' Later in the same article he said, 'From all that I've seen and heard of him, he is strong and aggressive. He hates losing and plays his cricket with real bravado. He has that touch of arrogance that you need at the top. Going for Irani would galvanise Darren Gough and Dominic Cork. They would both respond to the competition from a young thruster like Irani.'

Now I have never believed most of the stuff written about me in newspapers, good and bad, but when someone like Ian Botham writes something like that you do rather feel like buying all the copies, opening them up at the appropriate page and leaving them where everyone can read it. It gave me a tremendous boost and, even though I got quite a lot of stick in the dressing room along the lines of 'Look out, here comes the thruster,' it was worth it.

Of course, the England selectors took not the slightest notice of Beefy's advice but they did select me to go on the A tour to Pakistan under the captaincy of Nasser Hussain and with my pal from Lancashire, Jason Gallian. I had to take double doses of painkillers to deaden the pain in my back but it was still a terrific experience, despite picking up a duck in my first match. I went on to achieve a career-best 5-19 in one of the build-up matches and scored two half-centuries in the four-dayers against Pakistan A.

We returned home just before Christmas and I thought, if I could start the season well, there might just be a chance that I'd finally make the step up to the full England team. They'd had a torrid time in South Africa and failed in the World Cup that followed in India and Pakistan. My former Lancashire coach David Lloyd had been drafted in as team manager to try to pick up the pieces. He'd always seemed to rate me when I was in the second team and I know he'd often pushed my case with Neil Fairbrother.

I rested up for a couple of months, going for regular sessions with Laurence Sandum, a martial arts expert and fitness trainer, and by pre-season I was raring to go. I was soon playing well and again the media were linking me with the England team. In those days no one from the England set-up phoned and said you were selected – you had to listen to the radio when you knew an announcement was going to be made. Finally, I heard the magic words: 'Ronnie Irani has been chosen in England's one-day squad to play India at the Oval.'

The next few days were a bit manic – fielding loads of phone calls congratulating me and asking for tickets, and trying to make sure I was well prepared physically and mentally. But the match itself turned out to be something of an anti-climax. I batted seven and made 11 and I never got the ball in hand because the Indian innings lasted only 17 overs because of rain. I was then promptly dropped for the next two ODIs. Little did I realise but this was the start of what proved to be something of a trend.

I went back to Essex feeling a bit perplexed and wondering if I was going to be a one-match wonder. However, our first game was the perfect opportunity to give the selectors another nudge – we were playing the tourists at Chelmsford. I kicked the door as hard as I could. I picked up four wickets in their first innings, including their new wonderkids Rahul Dravid and Sourav Ganguly, and did OK with the bat. It worked. The next thing I heard was that I was in the squad for the first Test, to be played at Edgbaston the following week. I was finally about to achieve a dream I'd had since first making my way at Heaton as a kid.

I joined up with the squad in Birmingham on the Monday but it wasn't until Wednesday, the day before the match, that

I knew I was in the team. I'd expected some kind of announcement in a team meeting but I happened to bump into Mike Atherton in the lift after lunch and he just said, 'By the way, you're picked tomorrow. Good luck.' It was somehow typical of him. We'd never hit it off at Lancashire and he'd not been particularly welcoming when I made my ODI debut, and now his 'good luck' sounded more like it should have been followed by 'you're going to need it' than wishing me a successful first Test. I'd always found him dour and, while I thought he was a fine batsman, his leadership skills left a lot to be desired.

There's a tradition that a player making his debut sits next to the chairman of selectors at dinner the night before the match. I was a bit apprehensive because I'd heard a lot of tales about Raymond Illingworth and most of them were negative. I knew he had been a great cricketer – captain of England in two Ashes-winning series – but from what I'd heard he could be a bit of a Tartar. The rumours from the tour of South Africa were that there had been quite a lot of friction between him and Atherton. I wasn't looking forward to what might be a couple of uncomfortable hours where I'd have to watch everything I said in case I put my foot in it. But then I realised I was being daft, creating problems in my mind before they really existed. I remembered Fil Mercer's advice to take people as you find them and not on their reputation and once again he was spot on. It turned out to be a most enjoyable meal.

I shook his hand and said, 'I'm pleased to meet you, Mr Illingworth.'

'No, lad. Call me Ray.'

I wasn't sure I felt comfortable doing that, so we settled on 'Chairman'.

He turned out to have a passion for all sports and had a fund of entertaining stories. Being from Pudsey in Yorkshire, he had lots of tales about the great Leeds United team built by Don Revie and especially their England centre-half Jack Charlton. I also discovered that Ray was a former team-mate of John Savage, who had been so helpful to me as second-team coach at Lancashire. And we talked endlessly about our mutual passion for league cricket. Despite all his success as a player and an administrator, Ray had always kept in touch with his local club sides and I understand that until very recently he was still mowing the pitch at Farsley Cricket Club ready for their Bradford League matches.

I had a great time and was sorry when the coffee came round. As we got up to go, he said, 'Good luck tomorrow, Ronnie. You come highly recommended by people in the game whose judgement I trust. I like your attitude and the way you play the game. Just go out and enjoy it. Be yourself and, most of all, don't be afraid. Go for it.'

I went off to my room feeling a million dollars. I'd had a great evening and tomorrow I would wear the England sweater, pull on the cap with the crown and the three lions on it, and walk down the steps at Edgbaston a fully fledged Test cricketer. For the only time in my life, I didn't sleep a wink all night. Normally I'd have a couple of beers over dinner the night before a big match to help me nod off but I didn't feel I could do that sitting next to the chairman of selectors. I wondered about a glass or two of wine but decided against it and stuck with mineral water. I lay in bed tossing and turning, visualising loads of different scenarios, some triumphant, some disastrous. Eventually I decided to give up the unequal fight and flicked through the TV channels and came across *The Shawshank Redemption*.

I'd heard about this movie everyone was raving about but I'd never seen it. I quickly became hooked and for an hour or so I stopped thinking about cricket. Or almost. I couldn't help identifying with Andy and Red's fight against the establishment and bullying, and cheering their eventual escape from prison. While playing second-team cricket for Lancashire could hardly be compared to serving a life sentence in jail, there had certainly been times when I thought I would never get away and that some people were out to break my spirit. I too had been in danger of accepting that's just the way things are. But now, this first Test would be my version of walking along that wide, sunlit beach and believing there was another, better way.

CHAPTER 11

WELL DONE, YOU'RE DROPPED

By the time Mike Atherton threw me the ball to bowl, Sachin Tendulkar, who was just reaching the peak of his considerable talent, and the stylish Mohammad Azharuddin were threatening to put on a bit of a partnership. However, my fifth ball for England – not a particularly good one I will admit – tempted Azharuddin to have a swish and instead of racing for four it was brilliantly caught by Nick Knight.

If I'm completely honest, my back problems meant my bowling was not quite up to Test standard but I felt as though it was improving and I just concentrated on bowling tight. We dismissed the Indians for a little over 200 and looked very healthy overnight at 60 without loss, but on the second morning wickets started to tumble. Nasser Hussain, who was making his Test comeback after three years in the wilderness, was battling away, although he was fortunate to still be there. He had gloved one down the leg side to the keeper early on but got away with it when umpire Darrell Hair turned down a jubilant appeal.

He went on to score a priceless century and he and I

produced the vital stand that put things back on an even keel. I was nervous as I made what seemed a longer than usual walk to the crease but I quickly got off the mark and settled into it. I liked being out there in the centre of the arena in front of a big crowd, knowing the TV cameras were on me. It felt right. I hit 34 off as many balls. It all went by in a flash. I was playing shots but without really being conscious of what I was doing. I started to feel really good and wondered if a half-century and maybe more was on the cards but then I got a quick delivery from Javagal Srinath that got up a bit. I failed to drop my hands, it clipped me on the way through and was taken by the keeper.

Still, we won the game comfortably in under three days. I felt I'd contributed to the victory and was buzzing, but, when I went back into the dressing room after the presentations, everyone was just packing up and leaving. It was all so matter of fact. I had been hoping to sit around with the lads over a few beers and savour winning my Test debut; instead, they were all shooting off home. I packed my bag, slipped a bottle of presentation champagne in with my England sweater, and within an hour I was on the M6 making my way back to Essex. It was something of an anti-climax but I guess it reflected the way Mike Atherton liked things done. I just hoped I'd made a big enough impression to be selected for the next Test, which would fulfil another dream – to represent my country at Lord's.

I still wasn't sure I was playing until I saw my name on the team sheet and it turned out to be an incredibly memorable match, mainly because of Jack Russell, a great wicketkeeper, nice guy, top-class painter and complete eccentric. I'd heard a lot about him on the circuit, not least that he was very superstitious and would never change any of his kit. His floppy old sun-hat that had survived a fire, his patched-up gloves, even his vest and tatty old jockstrap had to be continually washed and reused long after they should have been chucked in the dustbin. He insisted on using the same tea bag for all five days of a Test match and his diet seemed to consist of mainly beans and rice.

My favourite story was of how protective Jack was of his privacy. Even his Gloucestershire team-mates didn't know where he lived, and rumour had it that he was so paranoid someone would follow him home that he would drive round a roundabout two or three times just to make sure no one was on his tail. One day he was asked to drive a young player to a match and, being a good team man, he agreed. But it gave him a dilemma because he had to go home first and collect some kit so he actually blindfolded the lad so he wouldn't know where he was going and only let him take it off when they were four or five miles away from the house.

Jack's ritual at matches was that he had to have two Weetabix soaked in milk for eight minutes at the close of play and, if he were batting, it was the twelfth man's job to prepare them. God help them if they were a minute out either way, because Jack could tell and would play hell.

The Lord's match started with an emotional entrance by the great Harold Dennis 'Dickie' Bird, who was in tears as he made his way to the wicket to umpire his last Test. He received a standing ovation, which is more than can be said for England. We made a dreadful start, the captain out for a duck with only one run on the board. But with Graham Thorpe making a solid knock we recovered and had scored over 300 when Jack was last man out, having hit his second Test century.

It looked a decent score until the Indians started to run riot over the next two and a half days. Ganguly and Dravid both made big scores on their Test debuts and helped them establish a big lead. I bowled very economically and picked up the wicket of Ajay Jadeja, and between innings David Lloyd made a point of telling me I'd bowled intelligently. It didn't look as though we could win the game but there was a grave danger we would lose it if we were dismissed cheaply in our second innings. Alec Stewart, who was fighting for his international career and only in the team because Nick Knight was injured, gave us a reasonable platform overnight but he was dismissed early on the fifth day and wickets started to tumble. We were six down when Jack Russell came out to join me in the middle.

'We're only 85 in front, Ronnie,' he said. 'It's up to us. We need runs but we must also make sure we don't get out.'

For me it meant playing against my natural game. I liked to attack the bowling and, while I was able to pick up some runs and had the occasional swish, most of the time I took no risks. Jack was like a stone wall. He must have been so frustrating to bowl against. Time after time it looked as though they would get the edge but he'd hop in the air and somehow withdraw his bat just in the nick of time. It was the most surreal innings I'd witnessed. He cracked one ball into the outfield and disturbed a group of pigeons as they pecked away at the seed. I set off for a run but Jack yelled, 'No! Go back! I can't see. Pigeons.' Then he called down to Dickie Bird, 'Dickie! Dead ball. Pigeons. Can't see.' Dickie obviously only heard the last part and got out his light-meter to check if it was too dark to play.

Later on, Srinath bowled a peach of a delivery that cut back and I thought rapped Jack on the thigh pad. He went down like a sack of spuds, clutching his knackers and groaning loudly. I ran over and asked him if he was OK.

'I'm fine but I can get five or six minutes out of this and it will help save the match.'

Dickie Bird shuffled up, clearly concerned, and Jack started to groan even louder. Srinath came over and said to me, 'No, no, no. This is no good. I know Jack. He's just pretending. If I had really hit him in the balls he wouldn't be able to make that much noise.'

Dravid and Ganguly looked on completely bemused. This wasn't anything like they had imagined Test cricket would be.

By now the twelfth man was on with some water. Jack took his time, walking up and down between sips. 'Come here,' he said to the twelfth man, who looked a bit apprehensive about what he was going to be asked to do. Then I heard Jack add, 'You'll have to re-time the Weetabix now because of this delay.'

I got out to one that kept low but we'd put on 60 and made sure the game was safe. I felt good because I'd played my part in helping us salvage a draw. I watched the highlights on TV and it was satisfying to hear the comments about my contribution. Geoffrey Boycott said that I'd shown character, and added with that familiar Yorkshire twang, 'I'm impressed with Ronnie Irani. If he has a day when things go well for him, he could do a lot of damage. There's a bit of Botham about him.' And Richie Benaud, one of the people my dad insisted I should always listen to, said he felt I'd already done enough to start packing my bags for the winter tour of New Zealand.

We made our way up to Trent Bridge and I unpacked all my gear at the hotel ready for the final Test. We knew we couldn't lose the series and I was hoping to round off what had been a good start to my international career in some style. I always enjoyed playing in Nottingham and when we looked at the wicket it was its usual flat self, a real feather bed. I briefly allowed myself to visualise the scene as I celebrated my maiden Test century.

On the afternoon before the match, I discovered another of Jack Russell's passions. He drove me to look at Nottingham castle and then we stopped at what felt like dozens of military memorabilia shops in the town. Jack was a very enthusiastic collector, especially of medals, and urged me to take it up. 'It's a great investment,' he assured me and suddenly I realised why people joked that he had dug a moat around his house.

We got to the ground on the morning of the match and had a good warm-up. We were just about to go into a circle for fielding practice when David Lloyd and Mike Atherton called me over. I instantly knew what was coming. There's only one reason for the 'Have you got a minute?' shout at that stage of the preparation. I couldn't believe it. Inside my head I was screaming, 'No! Fucking no!'

I could hardly take it in as Bumble's Accrington accent pronounced the verdict: 'Ronnie, you've done brilliant so far this series. You've done reeeally well. But we just want to take a look at Mark Ealham.'

'I don't understand,' I blurted out. 'We won the Test at Edgbaston and I helped save the match at Lord's. Why change it?'

'I know,' Lloyd said. 'You've done reeeally well, but that's just the way it is.'

Mike Atherton grinned sheepishly and shrugged. 'That's just how it goes.'

I knew it was no good arguing and said, 'So what do I do now?'

Lloyd patted my shoulder. 'Go back and play for Essex, lad. Don't worry, I'm sure you'll get other chances.'

The crowd were starting to come in as I made my way from one of the best batting tracks I'd ever seen towards the pavilion. I had no problem with Mark Ealham getting a chance – he was a good player and had earned it – but I had the shirt and, to my mind, I deserved a run in the side as long as I didn't screw up. I was in tears as I collected my bag from the empty dressing room. Then I had to go back to the hotel to pack my overnight gear.

Essex were just down the road at Leicester, so I phoned Paul Prichard from the hotel and told him what had happened. He couldn't believe it but said, 'Come down to Grace Road and we'll put you in the side.'

Before I knew it I was padded up but, instead of performing on a dream pitch in front of thousands, I was walking out to bat in front of a handful of people on a real sticky dog of a track. I was mentally fucked. I got a duck in both innings amid a torrent of sledging from the Leicestershire players about whether or not I was wearing the right sweater. 'Shouldn't that have three lions on?' the bastards sniggered. It was the first time in my life that I hated playing a game of cricket.

Fortunately, my season didn't end there. I quietly cursed David Lloyd and Mike Atherton, and wondered if their decision had anything to do with my leaving Lancashire, but then I remembered John Bird telling me when I was working in Tesco that 'Success comes in cans' and when I looked puzzled, he added, 'Not in cannots.' I decided the only way I could really prove them wrong was by playing better than ever and redoubled my efforts for Essex.

We were proving to be a growing force in the one-day

game and by August we were just one match away from the final of the NatWest Trophy final at Lord's. We faced a tough semi-final in front of a full house at the Oval against a top Surrey side that included Alec Stewart, Graham Thorpe, Chris Lewis and Adam Hollioake. Stewie hit a century as they reached 275 off their 60 overs, though I recall he found it hard to get me away. We felt they'd fallen short of what they should have scored on a very good pitch. We lost Paul Grayson early on to an lbw but Graham Gooch got runs as usual and our overseas player Stuart Law was just coming into form and he picked up a rapid half-century. We were still exactly a hundred behind Surrey when I went in at number six. I smashed them around for a quick 52 and together with Rob Rollins saw us home. I thought I'd done enough to pick up the champagne for man of the match but David Gower gave it to his mate Alec Stewart. Never mind: while Stewie was left to drink what must have tasted rather flat bubbly in defeat, I was heading for Lord's and a final against, of all clubs, Lancashire.

I would love to report that I scored a hundred as we carried off the trophy after humiliating my former county, but that kind of thing happens more in movies than life. Instead, we were robbed by a crap umpiring decision and some good play by Lancashire. We started brightly enough on a pitch that was giving the bowlers a lot of help. Mark Ilott knocked over Mike Atherton early on and the very next ball rapped John Crawley on the pads. It was plumb in front but for some reason umpire David Shepherd decided to shake his head instead of raising his finger.

That was a major turning point. My old pal John went on to take the game away from us with a superb knock as wickets tumbled around him. I picked off two more of my mates, Jason Gallian and Graham Lloyd, and had the great satisfaction of nipping one back to Neil Fairbrother, the man who didn't think I was good enough to pick, and it knocked out his middle pole. I ran past him and I think he was expecting a load of abuse but I just smiled and gave him the silent treatment. They only scored 166 but we were never in the hunt. Peter Martin and Glen Chapple were moving it sideways and we collapsed. It was a massive blow to me and the hurt of that day lasted a whole year until we returned to Lord's and picked up the trophy the following summer.

Before that, however, I was given my first full tour with England and it turned out to be one of the most dramatic periods of my life.

CHAPTER 12

THERE'S SHIT ON THE END OF YOUR BAT

Three of my closest friendships started on this tour, and thank God they did, because, without Darren Gough, Graham Thorpe and the maverick known as Phil Tufnell, I don't think I would have got through it.

The tour was set to last four months, first in Zimbabwe for a warm-up series and Christmas, then down to New Zealand and a Test and ODI series. Fitness was obviously going to be a major consideration and the whole squad was taken for a pre-tour training session at the Barrington Centre on the Algarve. It was a great time for me and that's where the four of us hit it off big time. We all knew what was at stake because this was the build-up to an Ashes series in England the following summer and we all wanted to be part of that.

Goughie is a tough Yorkie, a top-class fast bowler with his county's traditional grit and a heart that fills his stuck-out chest. He has become a great mate and eventually joined me at Essex while I briefly joined him on *Strictly Come Dancing*. You know all you need to know about Graham from the fact that, although naturally right-handed, he became a left-

111

handed batsman as a kid because the boundary in his garden at home was shorter on a southpaw's leg side and it gave him an edge over his brothers. He was a great batsman and, despite his problems later on, he was the kind of guy you would want in the trenches with you. This was a particularly tough tour for him because his wife gave birth just before we left and he was torn about being away from home.

It is impossible to speak about Tuffers without smiling. I find it a little strange that one of the greatest left-arm spinners produced by England is better known for being 'King of the Jungle' and making people laugh on *A Question of Sport*, because, make no mistake, Tufnell was a terrific bowler. Left-arm, orthodox, he was streetwise and cagey, with great variation. He had a lovely loop, produced plenty of revs and hardly ever bowled a bad ball. And he loved his cricket with a passion. In any other country he would have been worshipped for his knowledge but such is cricket in England, he is ignored because he is a bit of a character and wouldn't play the establishment game. He'd occasionally have a beer or six too many, or be caught round the corner having a quick fag. He couldn't be relied on to pass the port in the right direction or to tug his forelock to some petty official, yet, used properly, he could have helped produce a new generation of great spin bowlers.

I was rooming with Tuffers and managed to shock him early on. One of the tips I'd picked up in New Zealand was to take an ice-cold bath after exercise to get rid of the lactic acid that causes stiffness. It wasn't something I told many people about because I knew I'd get stick, so I waited until Phil was out of the way then ordered some ice to be brought up to the room. The waiter brought one ice bucket. 'No, I need a lot more than that. At least five or six that size.'

The guy raised an eyebrow as if to say, 'I didn't think athletes drank that much in the middle of the day,' but he brought the ice and I poured it in the bath. I was just about to run the cold water when Tuffers returned.

He took one look at the bath full of ice and said, 'Reggie! I knew you were going to be a great roomy. Where's the beers?' (He'd picked up on the fact that some of the Essex lads called me Reggie, as in Reggie and Ronnie Kray.)

'What beers?'

'For the bath. What a great idea. I'd never thought of it.'

'No, it's not for beer,' I explained. 'I'm going to get in it.'

I think he would've been less shocked if I'd told him that I'd just had a sex-change operation.

'Fuck me,' he said. 'What a waste.'

As I took my bath, I heard him on the phone to my team-mates: 'You'll never guess what this daft tosser's doing,' he said. 'The hairy-arsed bugger's getting in a bath full of ice!'

I think it's fair to say I was the butt of most of the jokes that night.

Tuffers hated the Algarve. 'Reggie,' he'd say, 'this place is doing my fucking head in. There's nothing to do. It's driving me nuts.' He'd wake me up in the middle of the night and say, 'Reg, I can't sleep. It's too fucking quiet. Talk to me, Reggie.'

He was right: there wasn't much beyond a golf course, a swimming pool and training, but physio Wayne Morton and fitness coach Dean Riddle were working us hard in training so I was quite content just to sit and chat between sessions and let my body recover.

I'd been keeping myself fit since I was 14 years old and it had become as much a part of my life as eating and looking for the Manchester United result. I even used to go out for a run every Christmas Day just to get an edge on the other guy.

As I ran, I would imagine all my rivals stuffing themselves with Christmas pudding and piling several pounds on to their waistline while I was putting a bit more stamina in the reserve tank. It was more psychological than physical but it worked for me.

As long as I wasn't struggling with injury, no coach could push me harder than I would push myself and on this trip I was feeling great. This was a chance to show Atherton and Lloyd they should never have dropped me at Trent Bridge and that, if I got my way, they would never get the chance to leave me out again. Chris Silverwood was renowned on the circuit for his fitness and I was up with him in almost every activity. He and I teamed up for the triathlon – swimming in the pool, cycling and running – and we won it comfortably. I was flying.

As a junior member of the squad, you are always keen to impress and hope that nothing is going to come up to put you into direct conflict with the management. You are bound to disagree from time to time but mostly you just accept that it's their job to make the decisions and you bite your tongue. The problem comes when they make a decision you disagree with and then make the mistake of asking your opinion. In those circumstances you have a straight choice between lying through your teeth to please them or telling them what you think and risk being tagged a rebel. We had one of those situations towards the end of the Algarve trip.

Apparently, the previous year's tour of South Africa had been a bit of a nightmare in terms of players' wives, even down to the England team bus being kept waiting to go back to the hotel after a match because a couple of wives were finishing their drinks. To me that smacked of poor management – either hire two buses or do what any sensible person would do, leave them behind to get a taxi. But the recently divorced Lloyd and unmarried Atherton had thought it over and announced at a team meeting that wives would be banned from this tour.

'We want to concentrate on the cricket, no distractions at all,' Bumble said. There was a murmur of complaint but it would probably have just stayed as something the players moaned about among themselves if he hadn't uttered those fateful words: 'What do you think?'

No one was anxious to put forward their point of view.

'Come on, what do you think? I want to hear from all of you.'

Most of the lads sat on the fence, especially when it became clear that any counter-argument was met with Lloyd or Atherton saying, 'I understand your point of view but we want to make sure we can concentrate 100 per cent on the cricket.'

Then it reached Goughie – if I remember rightly, the recently married Goughie. He spoke like he bowled, straight and hard: 'It's a fucking joke. You are completely wrong. Do you know how high the divorce rate is among cricketers? And it's mainly because we spend so much time away from home. I've just got married and, if I'm away for four months without seeing our lass, I'll need someone to introduce us all over again.'

'But, Darren, we want to focus on the cricket.'

'I'll focus on my cricket. I always focus on my fucking cricket. I can still do that *and* see my wife. We do it other times – what's so different about a bloody tour?'

Then it came to my turn. I was technically still single but I certainly didn't relish the thought of going four months without seeing Lorraine. I realised that nothing we would say would change their minds but I felt I had to say what I thought. 'I agree with Darren,' I said. 'He's got a good point and, if things are organised right, I don't see that having wives out there with us would make any difference to the way we play.'

It was a lost cause and the outcome was that a number of marriages suffered after that tour. It was bound to happen. Situations crop up when you are apart for that length of time and it's impossible to sort them out together. It's hard for players to pick up the routine of home life again after a long spell away in hotels with a bunch of blokes, and it's hard for their wives, who have had to cope with everything while they are away, to suddenly go back to having someone around who expects to be part of the decision-making process. People say, 'What about the forces?' and I agree it must be even tougher for them to handle but the difference is that, while it is impossible to take a wife into a war zone like Iraq or Afghanistan, there is absolutely no reason why she shouldn't be with her husband when he's taking part in nothing more dangerous than a cricket match.

It was a bad decision. There are lots of tedious times on tour, especially when you are not playing, and having families there would have helped that situation. As it was, we were a group of guys together and as a result we probably all drank a little too much that tour. I probably did more than my fair share, just because of the way things turned out while we were away, and I came back with the makings of a drink problem.

The other commandment handed down from the management was that we were not to fraternise with the enemy. Sorry, that should be opposition. But the mistake is easily made because David Lloyd certainly seemed to see this trip as some kind of military operation. I'm all for a 'never say die' attitude on the field, with no quarter given to your opponents, but I remembered that Viv Richards had told me I should always have a beer with them afterwards and, if it was good enough for Sir Viv, it was good enough for me. I was twelfth man in the first warm-up match and while my team-mates were in the field there was no one else to talk to, so I chatted to David Houghton and some of the other Zimbabwe lads, and great guys they were too.

I played in the second warm-up game and was pushing myself hard to bowl fast on a flat track when I felt my back go. A searing pain shot through me as though someone had plugged me into the electric mains. I walked straight off to the dressing room and knew it was bad. Wayne Morton asked what was wrong and I simply said, 'My back's gone. I'm fucked.'

'You can't say that. It may not be as bad as you think.'

He examined me thoroughly and, while he didn't say so, he obviously thought I was right because he advised the management to send for a replacement and Craig White was flown out from an England A tour. Craig was a good player, a bit quicker than me as a bowler but I always thought I had him covered as a batsman and I reckoned there was still a long way to go on the tour, so, if I could get my back sorted out, I could probably still get my place in the team. I told Wayne that I'd had the problem before and it had been sorted out by an injection straight into the L5 vertebra. He wasn't keen and told me it was risky but I begged him. 'Wayne, this is my big chance to play for England. If I don't take it this time, it may never come round again. Please, mate, it's worked before, it could work again. Please set it up. If it doesn't work, I'll go back to Essex and start again, but I have to give it a shot.'

Finally he agreed. We went to a hospital in Bulawayo but it was very basic and Wayne wasn't comfortable there. They kept us hanging around for a couple of hours before anyone came to see us and, after finally talking to the doctor, Wayne decided we would pass. 'Don't worry,' he said. 'I've heard of a specialist in Harare. We'll go and see her.' There was no plane scheduled for the next few days, so I pushed Wayne into driving. It took five hours and was agony most of the way despite the painkillers. Wayne insisted on playing Fine Young Cannibals tracks most of the way. 'She Drives me Crazy' almost drove me crazy but I was willing to put up with even that – I was that desperate to get it sorted out.

The hospital in Harare was in complete contrast to the one in Bulawayo, very modern and with all the latest equipment. The specialist gave me the injection and I could feel straight away that she'd hit the spot. The pain eased immediately and so did my concerns about my future on the tour. We had managed to book on a flight back and Wayne drove like Starsky and Hutch to get to the airport on time but when we reached the gate they told us the flight had been cancelled. They gave no reason and, with the sun shining from a clear sky, it certainly wasn't the weather.

'Why has it been cancelled?' Wayne demanded.

'It just has,' came the unconcerned reply. A little more clarity or even an apology might have prevented Wayne blowing his top, but I doubt it.

'You can't just cancel a flight for no reason,' he stormed. 'What kind of country is this? I want to see the boss. I want to see the man who decided to cancel our flight. We've got a big international cricket match coming up. Robert Mugabe will be at the ground. What do you think he will say when I tell him how you treated us?'

That seemed to strike a chord. We were led through to the back office where this huge guy sat behind a desk that must have left a clearing in the forest big enough to build a small village when they cut down the trees to make it. He looked as though he could handle himself and had two broad-shouldered minders just outside the door of his office. I started to get concerned that if we cut up too rough we could find ourselves beaten up and slung in jail. The words 'rubber glove' jumped into my mind. I whispered my doubts to Wayne.

'Don't worry, Ronnie, they won't mess with us.' Wayne made sure he spoke loudly enough for everyone to hear. 'There would be an international incident if they did and they won't want that.' Turning to the man behind the desk, he asked, 'Are you in charge round here?'

'Yes I am.'

'Did you cancel our flight?'

'Yes I did.'

'Well, you had no right. We've come here to play cricket and help promote your country around the world. Your president is coming to the match and we need to be in Bulawayo.' He slammed the desk as he emphasised, 'Tonight!'

The airport official didn't blink. He just sat there calmly smoking a cigarette.

'Look, I'm serious,' Wayne went on. 'You had better lay on a flight for us in the next half-hour or you can start looking for a new job.'

The man sucked on his cigarette, picked up the phone and in less than half an hour we were climbing aboard a smart private jet. As we settled into our seats, Wayne smiled at me sheepishly and admitted, 'I can't believe I did that.'

We had a very pleasant flight back to Bulawayo and within a couple of days I was able to resume training.

That wasn't the only flight Wayne and I had in a light plane on that tour. Our hosts had laid on a sightseeing trip for the squad to fly over the Victoria Falls. While the rest had modern aircraft, Wayne, Darren Gough and I had an old crate that looked like something out of *Murphy's War*. The view of the falls was unforgettably spectacular but the trip back rather took the gloss off the day. We hit a storm and the plane rattled and shook so much I thought every rivet must fall out. I was convinced we would all die. We eventually limped back to the airport but my legs were still shaking for a good hour after we touched down.

I was fit enough to be selected for the first ODI where, like the rest of the team, except perhaps Nasser Hussain, I struggled as we slipped to a two-wicket defeat. Two days later, Craig White was preferred to me for the first ever Test between the two countries. Watching from the sidelines, it became clear that, while Zimbabwe were the minnows of international cricket, they had a few top players, not least Grant Flower and his brother Andy, who later became my Essex team-mates. Andy was sheer class and scored a great century in that match. Nasser and John Crawley also scored tons and, while England had been expected to romp to victory, we were held to a draw. When Nick Knight was run out on the final ball with the scores level, Zimbabwe celebrated as though they had won, even though they had only scraped the draw by bowling as wide as they could without being signalled. Their joy at not being beaten clearly upset David Lloyd, who instead of being gracious said, 'We murdered them,' in his press conference. That remark didn't endear us to our hosts and their fans.

The papers back home gave Mike Atherton a lot of stick for not being able to polish off the weakest team on the international circuit, and the management decided to cancel the traditional Christmas party with the journalists who were following the tour. It was a petty decision – most of the stuff they objected to was done by editors back in London, not by the guys in the press box – but a pattern was beginning to emerge of a siege mentality from Lloyd and Atherton when they were put under pressure. What the players didn't realise at the time was that the ECB were concerned that the tour was turning into a shambles and the visit by the chairman Lord McLaurin was to bollock the management, not cheer on the troops.

With no wives allowed, Christmas turned out to be a miserable affair. The management didn't even arrange a Christmas dinner for the squad so Thorpe, Tufnell and I ended up in a hotel bedroom tucking into take-away from KFC and Pizza Hut and playing endless games of Balderdash. We were getting a reputation as being a bit of a clique. Mike Atherton made a few barbed comments and some of those at the front of the bus used to click their fingers whenever we made our way to the back. I felt that was unfair. When it came to training or playing, no one could doubt our commitment to the badge and the team, so what was the problem if we chose to spend our spare time together? Sports teams are made up of all kinds of different individuals. You have a lot in common with some of your team-mates and very little with others. That doesn't mean you wouldn't run through a wall for them in a match. Just as I'm sure Mike Atherton would have hated the idea of hanging out with me, I preferred to be with Thorpe and Gough.

Andrew Caddick was also part of our group. He's an

intelligent man, who knows his stuff and could be a fantastic bowler on his day. He also beats my missus all day long at ironing. There's not a piece of Caddy's clothing that hasn't been ironed immaculately, and he's such a good-hearted guy, he even volunteered to press a couple of my shirts when I was going out.

Alec Stewart was another who liked to have a good laugh. He would stir the pot a bit with his remarks and then duck out leaving others to sort it out. But he could take being teased too and took some stick about his superstitions. One day as the bus drew up at a ground, Graham Thorpe said to me, 'Check out Stewie.' Sure enough, as soon as the bus stopped, Alec was at the door with a small bag that he always carried with him. While the rest of us got our 'coffins' out of the baggage section, he was already in the dressing room claiming the spot he wanted. He was especially keen to have the same peg if he'd played at the ground before and done well. By the time we reached the dressing room, his stuff was set out immaculately, everything perfectly aligned. Mine was chucked in the first corner I came to.

Alec hovered between the front and the back of the bus, by nature one of the lads but not wanting to piss off the management too much. Nasser Hussain was also a bit torn on this trip because, while he enjoyed our company, he was vice captain for the first time so felt he had to toe the party line and not be seen hanging around too much with the clique.

I was left out of the second Test, which started on Boxing Day and also ended in a draw. But I was starting to feel strong once more and during the Test I received a fantastic masterclass in bowling from Ian Botham. He was covering the series for Sky TV and volunteered to give me a hand with my action, which I was trying to modify in order to protect my back. Just the fact that one of the legendary all-rounders with nearly 400 Test wickets to his credit was willing to spend time helping me, a novice with just two Tests and a couple of victims to my name, gave me a boost. Ian had great self-belief and confidence which was infectious, but he also had a lot more technical understanding than people give him credit for. At that stage I had been a professional cricketer for seven years and I can honestly say that was the best bowling coaching session I'd had. As I shook hands with Ian and went off to have a shower, John Emburey, who was the bowling coach on the tour, said, 'You're right again, aren't you?'

'Yeah, I feel really good,' I replied.

As it turned out, this was not my only coaching session from a legend. Geoffrey Boycott walked past the nets when I was batting and said, 'What's up with you?' I told him I'd had a back problem but that I was now close to full fitness and he replied, 'Good, because some of this lot are a waste of time – no heart and no bottle. Some of them can't bat for toffee.'

I'd known Geoffrey since he'd approached me during the final against Lancashire at Lord's. He'd stuck his hand out and said, 'All right, lad? I must admit, I like the way you play. I like your attitude. Bloody good cricketer.' As I started to preen, he smiled and said, 'Do you know what, though? I'd have loved batting against you. I'd have batted all day and you'd never have got me out.'

I was feeling a bit cocky because I'd taken on some of the greats like Brian Lara and Graeme Hick that summer and got them out, so I said, 'I only get good players out, Geoffrey.'

He gave me a big smile. 'You only get fucking good players out? In that case, you'd have got me first and second innings because I was a fucking good player.'

There was no arguing with that so, when the great man offered to take a look at my batting, I jumped at the chance. I arranged an extra session in the nets with Wayne Morton bowling to me. Wayne fancied himself as a bit of a medium-pacer and to be fair he would have probably been a reasonable bowler in the Yorkshire leagues, which are, of course, a step or so below their Lancashire equivalents. The nets were very wet after a downpour and had lots of grass on them but I thought I'd be OK against Wayne.

Geoffrey came over in his beige suit and Panama hat and said, 'You ready, Irani? Get down there and let's see what you've got.'

Wayne took out a brand-new Kookaburra, ran up and whipped one down to me which I got nowhere near. A sighter. I played and missed the second and the third knocked over my off stump. Boycott stood at the other end, impassive.

I got an edge to the next ball – straight on to my middle stump – and one of cricket's legends strolled down the wicket and said, 'Are you taking the piss out of me, Irani?'

'No! What do you mean?'

'I could bat against him without my pads.'

I mumbled something about the wicket and the fact that he had a new ball, but that well-known voice cut across me: 'New fucking ball? My grandma can bowl better than him. Now stop wasting my time and get on with it.'

By now a few people had spotted Geoffrey and were standing around to see what the great man had to say. He warmed to his audience and a couple of balls later yelled down the pitch, 'You've got some shit on the end of your bat, lad.'

I picked up my bat and looked at the end of it which was caked with mud. As I cleaned it off, he called out, 'No, Irani, the other end!'

I realised it was one of his favourite lines and just laughed. I knuckled down and the next 20 minutes were among the best I had with a batting coach. He spotted little things that made a big difference and when I put them into practice he'd say, 'Good technique that, good technique.'

I thanked him at the end of it and he replied, 'Any time, son. I like your attitude. Different class from some of these others.' I hoped that had been loud enough for the small crowd to hear and maybe it would even get back to the management.

Trying to bed in a new action until it becomes automatic takes a lot of hard work and time, so I wasn't too dismayed when I only performed averagely in the final two ODIs. Both were won by Zimbabwe with the Flower brothers again leading the way. Andy showed he was as hot behind the sticks as he was in front of them with a reaction stumping that sent me trailing back to the dressing room for nought.

We were all disappointed that we hadn't won a single international match on the tour so far but, free of pain and with a new action beginning to groove, I was looking forward to the next stage of the trip when we boarded the plane to New Zealand. It turned out to be a nightmare.

CHAPTER 13

WE'RE THINKING OF SENDING YOU HOME

It was a good job the press lads didn't see us when we reached our hotel in Auckland. The journey had taken the best part of 30 hours and we were completely knackered – far too weary to sleep – so we just dumped our bags and made for the bar. As I remember, several of us got hammered, including our captain, Mike Atherton. It felt like a ritual dumping of the disappointment of Zimbabwe and anticipating the rest of the trip. We had the next day off and I think most of us spent it in bed, shaking off our hangovers and catching up on sleep.

I couldn't wait for this part of the tour to get under way. I liked New Zealand and was looking forward to meeting up again with the Lucas family and other friends I'd made on my previous stay there. I was pain-free and raring to go. I knew I had a lot of competition for my place – Craig White was still with us and Dominic Cork had arrived after sorting out some domestic problems that made him pull out of the Zimbabwe leg. But I was firing on all cylinders. I was bowling long stints in the nets and knocked over Mike Atherton's off stump a couple of times. I also did well against Nasser Hussain and Alec Stewart and was one of the best performers in a practice match among ourselves. With a couple of warm-up games before the Tests to come, I felt my form was peaking at the right time. I was desperate to show what I could do.

Not everyone was feeling as good as I was. In Atherton's first press conference in New Zealand, Michael Nicholson of ITN asked, 'When are you going to do the decent thing and resign?' Ath had been struggling with a back injury and was badly out of form. With that and poor team results, the knives had been out for him since just before Christmas and he was a bit shaken when Nicholson added, 'If you were the chief executive of a public company, you would have been kicked out by now.'

Bumble was also feeling the pressure after ECB chief executive Tim Lamb stated, 'Lord McLaurin and I were horrified by what we saw in Zimbabwe. We were not happy with the way the England team presented themselves. Their demeanour was fairly negative and not particularly attractive.' That might go some way towards explaining the management's overreaction shortly after we arrived in New Zealand.

One by one, the whole squad was called into a meeting with Lloyd, tour manager John Barclay, Mike Atherton and John Emburey and asked how they thought the tour was going. When the question was put to me, I replied, 'Obviously it's not been great for me so far. I was gutted when I did my back in but we've got it sorted out now. I'm feeling good and looking forward to the games coming up. I'm really up for it.'

Lloyd shook his head and said, 'I'll tell you exactly what's happened to you. You came on tour unfit. You've hidden behind injury after injury. You are injury-prone and you have covered up from the start. You are a disgrace. You are one of those players who is always in the physio's room with some niggle or other. You know what? I'm banning you from seeing the physio again. It's not good enough.'

I was stunned. I couldn't believe what I was hearing. For a while, my head was spinning, trying to make sense of what he'd said. I looked at the others. John Barclay looked nervous, and Mike Atherton and John Emburey wouldn't look me in the eye. I could feel my fury welling up but I forced myself not to jump in and protest too angrily.

As calmly as I could, I replied, 'With all due respect, I did not come away injured. If you remember, I finished the season at Essex fully fit and played in the Lord's final. If you look at my record at the end of the season, I bowled loads of overs and made runs – I couldn't have done that if I wasn't fit. For God's sake, when we were in the Algarve, I won the triathlon with Chris Silverwood. Does that suggest I was covering up an injury? Until I did my back in Zimbabwe I was playing well. You saw that. I don't understand how you can accuse me of coming away unfit.'

'I'll tell you how,' Lloyd said. 'I've got a list here of every time you've been to see the physio. You've had problems with your back, trouble with your hamstring, niggles in your side, your shoulder and your knees.'

'Sure, but all bowlers have that. It doesn't stop you playing. You have some treatment and then you go back out there and perform. You must know that. But what happened in Zimbabwe was different – it was impossible for me to play until I had the injection.'

'No. As far as I'm concerned, you came on this trip unfit and it's not good enough.'

I was getting desperate now. 'I would never lie just to get on tour. You've known me since I was a kid, I can't believe you would say that. I was fine – I just injured my back in Zimbabwe and had to get it fixed.'

The rest of them sat there like the three wise monkeys. I couldn't believe that Atherton didn't speak up when he'd also been nursing a bad back all the way through. I was about to say that but stopped myself. No point in antagonising them by attacking a member of *their* clique. Somehow I had to try to retrieve the situation. It was clear I wasn't going to change Lloyd's mind, so I decided to try to move it on to something more positive.

'David,' I said, 'you are the boss and I have to respect what you say, but you also know that I've had my injection, I've been working my guts out with Dean Riddle and Wayne Morton. I had a great session with Ian Botham to iron out some problems in my technique. Embers, you commented how much I'd improved. I've been putting in extra shifts in the nets and I've done well in practice games. I've bowled my heart out.'

Lloyd nodded. 'Yeah, you've done well.'

'I feel really good now. I'm up for it. I was first-choice all-rounder when you picked the squad and all I'm asking for is a chance.'

'We'll see.'

And that was it. I left the room angry, confused and despondent. I wanted to scream with frustration, to punch something or someone. I was appalled at the injustice of it – I was being made a scapegoat for the failures of the tour, punished for picking up an injury while doing my job. I'd longed to play for my country again but now it looked as though it would never happen and I didn't understand why. I got back to my room, raided the mini bar and poured myself a stiff drink. I just wanted to catch the first plane home.

Not long afterwards, there was a knock on the door and when I opened it Mike Atherton was standing there. 'I've come to tell you that we have two warm-up games and then the Tests and you won't be playing in any of them. Craig White will play in all of them.'

Just like that. All the effort I'd put into getting myself ready for this leg of the tour counted for nothing. 'Mike,' I protested, 'I've obviously got some problem I don't understand but I was first-choice all-rounder at the start of this trip. Why can't I play in one of the warm-up matches and prove that I'm ready to play?'

'It's not going to happen. It's been decided and that's just the way it is.'

I was completely shattered. I told Phil Tufnell, Graham Thorpe and Darren Gough and they couldn't believe it. I said, 'You guys have been with me all the time. Tell me, what have I done?'

They had no answer. They were sympathetic and supportive, as was Nasser who commented, 'I don't know what it is, Ronnie, but for some reason Bumble has taken against you. Whenever you are mentioned, he is always critical.'

I had virtually been told I had three weeks off. I worked my bollocks off every day in training, bowled in the nets morning and evening and took every opportunity to work with fitness coach Dean Riddle. Every night I went out and got hammered. They'd also told Jack Russell that Alec Stewart was keeping wicket so he too had three weeks off. I could tell he was frustrated but he went back to his room and got on with his painting commissions. He was at his happiest on his own with his paints and easel and preferred a cup of tea to alcohol, but one evening I went to his room to see if he fancied a night on the town. 'Why not?' he said. Once again, he was fascinating company with lots of great stories. We managed to make short work of a few bottles of a very nice New Zealand white wine, chatted to some of the Barmy Army and had a thoroughly good time. Jack is built like a jockey and at the end of the evening I lifted him over my head and carried him out of the bar.

The first Test was at Eden Park. After some stunning batting by Alec Stewart and Graham Thorpe and a super little cameo innings from Dominic Cork, England were cruising to victory when they took the ninth New Zealand second-innings wicket with the Kiwis only 11 in front. Danny Morrison, who was coming out to join Nathan Astle, held the world record for ducks in Test cricket, so I'm sure the bookies had already stopped taking any bets. But Danny chose this day to produce his finest batting performance. The two of them hit a record stand for the last wicket and managed to bat out the whole of the last day, turning certain defeat into a heroic draw. Morrison only scored 14 but just would not be shifted. The irony is that, after all his efforts, he was never chosen for his country again. Welcome to the club.

There were big question marks over Mike Atherton's tactics and the England dressing room was like a morgue. The mood hadn't improved when we boarded the team bus. Usually Graham Thorpe would take the microphone and do his wickedly accurate impression of Geoffrey Boycott – 'Good day, England. Bloody good day. Good creeckit' – but this time he just made his way to the back seats and sank down beside Phil Tufnell, me and some other members of the 'clique'. The spirit of the party was not helped when we were kept hanging about, which allowed a group of young New

Zealand fans to gather round and start shouting abuse at us. 'Wankers' was one of the nicer things they called us and I could tell Tuffers was starting to get upset.

'Fucking vultures,' he said. 'Why do people love to have a go?'

As the bus pulled away, the crowd jeered and Phil climbed up on the seat, dropped his tracksuit trousers and stuck his naked bum against the back window – the hairiest smile those guys are ever likely to see. The rest of us laughed, which made the management turn round. By now, Tuffers was fully dressed again and looking as innocent as a choir boy, so they didn't know why we were laughing and probably just assumed that we didn't care about the way the game had gone.

The next day I was summoned to see John Barclay. 'Ronnie, something has come to our attention that we take very seriously and I have to warn you that we are thinking of sending you home,' he said.

I thought, Fuck me, what have I done now?

'We think this is a serious breach of discipline and not what we expect of someone representing England,' he droned on.

I was racking my brains trying to think what dreadful thing I'd done. Admittedly I'd been pissed a lot in the last couple of weeks, but I'd never caused any bother in a bar and I'd always turned up on time for training and worked my socks off in the nets, even though I knew I had no chance of playing. And, surely, if it was the drinking, they'd have pulled me about it before?

'I don't know what you're talking about, John,' I said.

'I think you do, Ronnie.'

I thought, He's testing me. He's not sure and he's trying to trap me into confessing something that he thinks might have happened. I played as straight a bat as Danny Morrison. 'Honestly, I don't have a clue. What is it?'

'You were seen pulling a moonie on the team bus as it left the ground yesterday.'

'What!'

'You were seen dropping your trousers at the fans and the press. It is very serious.'

I knew he'd screwed up big time. I decided I wouldn't deny it for a bit and see where it took us.

'Who told you this, John?'

'I can't tell you that because it was told to me in confidence.'

'That's all very well,' I said, 'but you are threatening to send me home from an England tour in disgrace for something I didn't do. I think I have the right to know who told you.'

'You deny it?'

I was seething by now. 'John, get the person who told you I pulled a moonie to come here now and repeat it in front of me. I've got plenty of time. Get him here now.'

'Are you saying you didn't do it?' He was starting to look unsure of himself.

'I didn't. So let's see why your informant thinks it was me. Get the tosser in here now.'

'There's no need to be like that.'

'No need to be like that? Some anonymous twat tells you a tale and, before you've even checked, you are talking about sending me home. I think I've every reason to be like that.'

'If it wasn't you, who was it then?'

'John, I'm not going to drop one of my team-mates in it. I'm pissed off that someone came telling tales and I'm pissed off that you assumed he was right. It seems to be the general view on this trip that, if anything is wrong, it must be Ronnie Irani. Now will you get him in here?'

'I'll have a word with him and ask him if he'll come and talk to you.'

'That's not good enough, John. You are the team manager. *Tell* him to come. He could have wrecked my career and the least he can do is to see me face to face.'

I stormed out and headed back to my room, fuming.

'What's up with you?' Tuffers asked.

'Those bastards want to send me home.'

'Why? What have you done now?'

'They've accused me of mooning at the back of the bus.'

He hit the roof. 'The wankers! That was me. Right! They can send me home. Fuck 'em.'

'No, leave it. It's not worth it. Let them stew.'

We both had a beer and calmed down. We agreed the tour was being managed by clowns who had no idea how to handle grown men. To my mind, if there was going to be any punishment for showing your arse to abusive fans, it should be a verbal rap over the knuckles or a fine. They had completely overreacted. We spent the rest of the evening having a few drinks and laughing about it. But deep inside I was still incredibly angry. It was another sign that for some reason the management had decided I was the bad boy of the tour and were looking for any excuse to bomb me out.

The next day at the end of training, Malcolm Ashton, the tour scorer, came over to see me. We'd always got on well – he was the king of Balderdash – and I thought he'd probably got some stats I'd asked for.

'Ronnie, it seems I owe you an apology. I was the person who told the management. I thought mooning the public was out of order and should be reported. I didn't realise I'd got it wrong.'

I wasn't quite sure how to react for a second. Then I said, 'Malcolm, you can have your opinion about mooning but, as far as I'm concerned, you were bang out of order. You know what it's been like for me on this tour. I'm trying to carve out an international career and you nearly had me sent home for something I didn't do.'

He was full of apologies but I just walked away. I didn't want anything to do with him.

We won the second Test by an innings when Thorpey again came good. I was delighted for Graham. I'm still not sure how he managed it. He'd been a reluctant tourist who wanted to be with his new baby and spent most evenings on the trip getting hammered with Tuffers and me. The guy clearly had stamina as well as talent.

Mike Atherton finally found some form to clinch the third Test, but to be honest the whole tour was now so sour for me that it was difficult for me to care what happened in the matches. By the time the ODIs came round, I was mentally fucked. I wanted to be anywhere else but in New Zealand with England under a management for whom I no longer had any respect. I played in three of the matches, got a couple of wickets and ran one guy out, but I had a nightmare with the bat and was relieved when they left me out of the final game. I just wanted to get home and decide what I was going to do. Right then, my main thought was to pack the game in altogether.

CHAPTER 14

I WANT TO BE A MOUNTAIN PERSON

I've always loved those pithy little sayings that sum up how to make the most of life. You know the kind of thing: 'You can only control what's in your control'; 'When the pupil is ready, the teacher appears'; 'The way a man wins shows much of his character, the way he loses shows it all'. I often used them when I became Essex captain just to get an idea over to the team and some of the guys used to groan when I came out with a new one, but to me they helped instil a positive attitude.

It would have taken more than a whole bloody book full of them to make me positive when I got back from New Zealand. I must have been very hard to live with but again Lorraine was a rock and overlooked a lot of things that normally she would have complained about. I couldn't see any future. I didn't usually feel sorry for myself and, if I'd been objective, I'd have realised how fortunate I was compared to many people, yet I couldn't shake myself out of my gloom. I started to prepare for the new season at Essex by doing a bit of jogging but early on I suffered a panic attack while I was running. My throat seized up and I found it hard to breathe. It was very scary but I didn't tell anyone except Lorraine.

I talked to Graham Gooch and Keith Fletcher about the tour and both said they couldn't understand why the England management had given me such a hard time. They were very supportive but I was still unsure if I wanted to carry on playing cricket. I'd achieved my dream of representing my country and discovered it wasn't what I'd expected. Those boyhood fantasies of feeling proud to wear the three lions had been spoiled by a group of mean-spirited people who just wanted clones, not individuals with minds of their own. They wanted the equivalent of Stepford cricketers and that just wasn't me. I arranged to meet John Bird and made up my mind that, if he offered me an even half-decent job at Tesco, I would take it and turn my back on cricket. I think he realised how low I was and had the sense to understand that what I needed was help to cope with the situation, not an easy way out.

Bizarrely after all that had happened on tour, I was invited to meet up with the squad again for a 'team-building' session. It was run by former England rugby captain Will Carling and contained all the usual bollocks like trying to cross a river without getting your feet wet or helping each other climb up poles. To me, it was all a bit pointless – if you've got as far as being selected to play cricket for England, you should already know what it takes to be a team player and support your mates. But I was determined to show the management they had been wrong about me and, just as in the Algarve, I was among the fittest there. Graeme Hick had been invited to join the group and he was so fit he got the nickname Arnie after Arnold Schwarzenegger, but I matched him in most things, and each time I performed well I thought to myself, Who's injury-prone now?

On the second evening, we were all called together to listen to a motivational speaker. I was reluctant to go but I didn't want to give them any more ammunition to fire at me, so I went along. It turned out to be a great decision.

The speaker was Frank Dick, the former director of coaching for British athletics and the man who had helped Daley Thompson and Linford Christie to Olympic glory. He'd also worked with top performers in other sports like Boris Becker, Formula 1 driver Gerhard Berger and the figure-skater Katarina Witt. He had a presence about him as soon as he walked on the stage and grabbed my attention with his opening lines: 'There are two kinds of people in my world – valley people and mountain people.

'Valley people seek the calm and comfortable ground of shelter, safety and security,' he went on. 'They may talk about change, but do not want to be involved in it, especially if it means breaking from the routine of what's worked OK up till now. Their concept of achievement is "not losing", so playing for the draw to them is all that's needed. They are the people you meet whose sentences start with "I would have...", "I could have..." or "I should have..." They are the almost people who have many explanations for not making it themselves and only one for those who have – luck. They talk about the risk of losing and yet they are losers – they just don't know it.'

By now I was oblivious to everything and everyone around me. It seemed as if Frank was talking directly to me. It was as though he'd been by my side over the last few months, witnessed my turmoil and was now giving me solutions.

'Mountain people have decided that valley life is not for them,' he continued. 'And they seek to test ambition on the toughest climbs. They know that there is a rich satisfaction in reaching the top and the fight that's needed to get there. They live for the test of changes and enjoy the resilience required to bounce back from the bumps and bruises that come with the mountain territory. They not only talk about change, they deliver it.'

I was mesmerised all the way through his talk and again his comments might have been directed straight at me when he concluded, 'I believe that the game is there to be won – and that it's for *you* to do the winning.'*

I had to meet this guy. I went up to him afterwards and shook his hand. I wanted to ask him a thousand questions, tell him what I was going through and ask his advice but I wasn't sure if he was part of the England management structure. I didn't want them to know what I was feeling, so I just thanked him for a great speech.

But the more I thought about what he'd said, the more convinced I became that he could help me. He'd made me believe my career was worth fighting for, perhaps not with England but certainly with Essex where things had been going great and where I was appreciated by the management, the fans and my team-mates. I needed to talk to him but didn't know how to go about it, so I rang Medha Laud at the ECB, another of those people in the background who do so much work. The lads always loved her because she sorted things out without any fuss. She gave me Frank's number. I rang him and explained that I'd like to see him and discuss my career.

---

*These thoughts and many others that have helped change my life can be found in Frank's book *Winning: Motivation for Business, Sport and Life* published by Abingdon Publishing and reproduced here with his permission.

'No problem,' he said. 'Come to my home.'

That was the start of a friendship that has survived to the present day and helped shape my life. He, his wife Linda and their two daughters made me instantly welcome. Frank listened to my story and then not only helped me to deal with the disillusionment but also advised me how I could become physically fitter and stronger. It was as though I'd been given a transfusion of optimism and self-confidence. Suddenly I not only felt that I *could* be a top-performing cricketer, but I knew that I *would*. I couldn't wait for the season to start.

Two events stand out for me in what proved to be a successful season at Essex. The first was in the car park at Northampton when Graham Gooch took me to one side and said, 'Ronnie, I've only known you a few years but I feel quite close to you and I just wanted to let you know that I'm going to announce that I'm retiring today.' I was sad because I felt he still had a lot to offer on the pitch, but I also felt extremely proud and privileged that he had chosen to tell me personally. He moved up to a coaching position at Essex and continued to play an enormous part in my career.

The word 'legend' is bandied about too freely in the media but Graham is one of the few modern cricketers who deserves to have it attached to his name. His record as a batsman speaks for itself; he was a key member of Essex teams that won six county championships; he was a decisive and honest captain, leading by example; and he was a fantastic trainer – even when he was in his forties, many of us found it hard to keep up with his fitness regime. Above all, he was a deep thinker about cricket and was willing to share his thoughts with people he believed were really interested. Over the years at Essex, Keith Fletcher passed on all he knew to Goochie, and Graham passed it on to me. Nasser Hussain used to call me 'son of Fletch' or 'son of Gooch' in a sarcastic way but I looked on it as a badge of honour. It was a tremendous privilege to work with both of them.

The other major event was reaching the final of the NatWest Trophy for the second year in a row. After the disappointment of losing to Lancashire the previous September, we were all determined to make a better fist of it this time. But for a while it looked as though I might not get the chance. The semi-final was at Chelmsford against Glamorgan and, midway through my tenth over, I tore the intercostal muscle off my rib. It felt as though someone was grinding glass into my side. They gave me an injection and pumped me full of painkillers so I went out to bat as high as a kite. I was aware of the nagging pain in my side but didn't give a damn and went on to score 51 and see us to the brink of victory.

A lot was made of an incident when I was finally out lbw and I guess it looked bad on TV but was really nothing. The ball rapped me on the pad and I set off, head down, for a run. Halfway down the wicket, I met the bowler, Darren Thomas, who had just seen the umpire's finger go up and was punching the air as he turned back towards me. Instead of the air, he caught my helmet and knocked me to the ground. On TV it looked like a great right hook, but it was a complete accident and probably hurt Darren's hand more than it did me.

As we celebrated reaching Lord's, our physio James Davis broke the bad news: an intercostal injury would take six to eight weeks to fix. That just wasn't good enough. There was a Lord's final against Warwickshire in three weeks and I was desperate to have another crack at it. I remembered Frank Dick telling me about a wonderful doctor in Munich who looked after Bayern Munich and the German national football team and who had performed miracles on some of Frank's athletes. I decided I would go and see him. It was the first of many trips I made to the genius named Dr Hans-Wilhelm Müller-Wohlfahrt.

Over the next few days my body was like a dartboard. 'Healing Hans', as he was dubbed, explained that he didn't use steroids or painkillers, just amino acids to speed up the body's own healing process. 'Normally, your body takes what you eat, passes it through the gut into the blood and that goes to the injured area and repairs it. With a little rest and physiotherapy you get better. All we do is shortcut the system by supplying what your body would eventually create directly to the injured tissue. It speeds everything up.' Within two weeks, I was pain-free and felt perfectly fit.

I played in a four-day game in the week leading up to the final. I didn't risk bowling but I batted and fielded and it all seemed to be OK. We made our way to London to stay in the hotel next to Lord's before the match but it was London as we had never seen it. It was the weekend of Princess Diana's funeral and it was incredible to witness at first hand the outpouring of public grief. On the Friday night, Lorraine and I went out to look at the sea of flowers people had placed around Buckingham Palace and Kensington Palace. It was slightly unreal seeing people standing sobbing or hugging strangers, united in mourning for someone they had only known through their television and newspapers. The following day the funeral cars came past the door of our hotel on their way to her burial at Althorp. Lorraine and I were both in tears as we stood among the mass of people who had been waiting on the pavement for hours just to get a glimpse of the coffin. Even more flowers were strewn across the road, as if to cushion her final journey.

It was all incredibly emotional and somehow added to my nervousness later in the day when I had the fitness test to see if I could play in the final. Lord's was closed so the whole Essex team found a clear spot in Regent's Park for a final practice for the biggest match of our season! It was a bit like those pictures you see of the 1950s when kids put down coats to mark the wickets. It was impossible to bat but we did some catching practice and then measured out a rough wicket for me to test my ribs. I hadn't attempted to bowl since picking up the injury and was a bit apprehensive as physio James Davis taped me up but, as soon as I let the first ball go, I knew I was all right. I bowled for about 40 minutes with no reaction: I was ready to play.

I stiffened up overnight but a good warm-up and the adrenaline that kicks in when you play in a big event saw me through. I completed my 12 overs at the cost of just 22 runs and took a wicket as we restricted Warwickshire to 170. Paul Prichard and Stuart Law took us to the brink of victory and then Nasser helped Stuart finish the job. We'd made amends for the failure the year before and I had picked up my first winner's medal. After all the traumas of the winter tour, the doubts and fears when I got home and the drama of the last couple of weeks, it was one of the sweetest feelings I ever had. Now it was time to push on again.

CHAPTER 15

COCKSCOMB INJECTIONS

I've never understood why so many professional sports people act like spoiled brats and think they don't have to take any responsibility for their own welfare. Let's face it: playing sport is a pretty damn good way of life despite all the ups and downs, occasional frustrations and the odd bloody-minded management making things difficult. To start with, you are paid well to do something many thousands would pay to do. You get to travel the world and stay in good hotels with someone else picking up the tab. You even get perks now and again like invitations to big sporting events and drinking corporate champagne from the comfort of an executive box.

But it seems this isn't enough for some people. They start to believe they shouldn't have to pay for anything. I get angry when I hear a highly paid professional whinge that his club or association wouldn't pay for treatment he thought he should have. I want to say, 'You can afford to pay for it yourself. It's your career and your body you are talking about – take steps to sort it.'

There are, of course, some notable exceptions, and the more I looked into getting the best treatment I could find, the more I kept bumping into the same people who were willing to invest their own money in their own future – people like Jamie Redknapp, who has become a good mate and with whom I've spent a lot of time swapping stories about who is the best person to see for particular injuries.

My experience in New Zealand and with Hans Müller-Wohlfahrt convinced me how important it was to think outside the box and to seek out the best advice I could get, even if it cost me. I discovered an important truth: the people at the top of their profession don't bullshit you. If they need to refer you to another specialist, they always recommend the best because they know it reflects on them.

I played no cricket in the winter following the NatWest Trophy win. I had an operation on my right knee and started my regular visits to see Hans in Munich. He was definitely one of Frank's mountain people. He'd overcome enormous opposition from the established medical profession to his homeopathic treatments but his results spoke for themselves – literally, because most of his patients came from word-of-mouth recommendation by satisfied customers.

When I went to see him, he would put me on a drip of Actovegin, an amino acid created during a filtration of molecules of calves' blood. It makes you piss like a race horse but it gets rid of the toxins and you feel wonderful after it. Eventually the World Anti-Doping Agency felt it might be too easy to include other, less desirable substances in a drip so it had to be administered by injection. No one in England would give me the injections, so I took Lorraine to Munich where they showed her how to do it and for eight years she would give me the jabs in our bedroom at home. It was all perfectly legal and speeded up my regeneration incredibly. I had plenty of drug tests during this time but there was never a problem as all the treatments I used were homeopathic.

When he turned his attention to my knee, Hans used a substance called Hyalart and later Ostenil. Hyalart is processed from the comb of a cockerel. It stays on the surface of the skin for ages and seems virtually impossible to rub in, and it works miracles at lubricating the knee joint, preventing the bones grinding together. When the story eventually broke that I was having Hyalart injections, I had to put up with a lot of jokes and Ian Botham still insists that he finds it hard to understand how having a chicken's head shoved in your knee can help. But I was happy to put up with the mickey-taking because of the relief I got.

For the next few years, I used to take myself off to Munich at least once a month for treatment. At first I didn't tell anyone at Essex in case they thought it was too way out and stopped me. The schedule was always touch-and-go and it made me a keen student of weather conditions, especially the possibility of fog. I would fly out at 7.30am on a Monday and return the same night, ready for a game the following day. There were a few hairy dashes to the airport to make sure I didn't miss the plane but fortunately it always worked out OK. I was lucky because I lived near Stansted airport where I could get an Easyjet flight to Munich for around £120 and at times as little as £60. If I'd still been with Lancashire, it would have cost me £400 to fly from Manchester. Eventually, word got out and I know our physio James Davis was a bit sceptical at first but he came out and saw Hans's set-up for himself and became enthusiastic about it. And Essex were great. When they realised how much the treatment was helping me, Alan Lilley and David East contributed towards the costs.

It was thanks to Jamie Redknapp that I met Kevin Lidlow, one of the best physios in the world. After my knee operation, Hans Müller-Wohlfahrt would take away the swelling while Kevin would work on getting rid of the scar tissue left from my earlier operation. He was another guy whose reputation went from player to player. Most of his work is done in the Third Space clinic in London, but sometimes I would ring him during a match and he would tell me to go to his place in Stapleford when I got home. I've often turned up from somewhere like Durham at 10 or 11 o'clock at night and found people like Jamie, Les Ferdinand, Scott Parker, Joe Worsley or Lawrence Dallaglio sitting waiting their turn to go in.

By this stage, some of you may be thinking that I'm some kind of hypochondriac flitting from treatment to treatment, but you have to remember that, if you are doing your job properly as a sportsman, and in my case that meant batting and bowling on a daily basis, you are putting strains on your joints, your back and the rest of your body that most people don't experience. And I had been doing that from a very young age. Just as Formula 1 teams spend hours tuning their engines and going over every working part to make sure the car performs at peak levels, I reckoned I needed to treat my body with the same care. An athlete's body is not something a GP can look after satisfactorily; it needs specialists in several fields and I was extremely lucky in that I became part of a network that passed me on from one expert to another. It was expensive but it prolonged my career by several years.

One of the guys Hans introduced me to was Thomas Mendelssohn, a chiropractor who immediately spotted my neck, spine and hips were out of alignment and put them right, making bowling a whole lot easier. And he put me on to Martin Trautmann who updated my orthotics and later became a partner in OrthoSole, the product I launched in 2008 in the UK and at a massive trade fair in Salt Lake City in July 2009.

Back in 1997, I had plenty of time on my hands between treatments and, as soon as he heard I wasn't playing cricket that winter, Fil Mercer got in touch with me with a business proposition. Fil had managed to get a good price from Securicor for delivering parcels across his range of companies. On the ball as ever, he quickly realised there was enough margin for him to offer a reasonably priced parcel service to his friends and make a few bob for himself.

'Why don't you set up something similar in Essex?' he asked. 'I'll give you a good price and it will be a way for me to pay you back some of the money I owe you. All you need is a phone and a diary.'

It made sense so I started to help Parcels2Go.com in Essex and we did quite well. I could have continued with it but once my knee was fully fit and I was back playing there simply wasn't enough time. Anyway, by that stage I was making more money out of another scheme with Fil's brother Dougie, another Mercer who could duck and dive for England.

Dougie can be a bit flash and likes his sports cars – to my knowledge, he's had at least one Porsche, a Lotus and a Ferrari – but I'd known him for years and was happy to get on board when he asked me to sell a damp-proof membrane that builders put down over the foundations of buildings. Despite a few hiccups and a writ from a £100m company who felt we were making false claims for our product, sales were going well and I was building up a nice little business. An apology and promise not to repeat the claim dealt with the writ but there was no way past one of Dougie's main customers.

The guy complained that I was nicking his clients and threatened to close his account, which would have been disastrous for Dougie. I had a word with the bloke – or rather I had a row with him on the phone and took such exception to his threats that I offered to meet him and sort it out. He backed off at that stage and we agreed to rub along together as long as I didn't take any more of his customers.

I carried on selling for a few more weeks but, inevitably, without realising, I approached someone he usually dealt with and got an order. The guy instantly phoned Dougie, who came on to me and said, 'I'm sorry, Ronnie, but I've got a lot of people whose jobs depend on me and I can't afford to lose this bloke. I've got to ask you to stop completely.'

I wanted to argue – I was making some useful money that I needed right then – but I agreed to walk away. It wasn't worth losing a friendship over it. Dougie and I are still mates. He has gone on to do very well with his business and property portfolio in England and abroad, on the back of which he drives around in a Bentley convertible. I'm still in my Mondeo classic.

CHAPTER 16
ON YOUR BIKE

In many ways, 1998 was one of the more forgettable years of my life. Only two occasions stand out as memorable – my wedding and another trophy with Essex in the B&H final.

I like to think I'm a decisive kind of bloke but I have to admit that it took me ten years to get round to proposing to Lorraine. It didn't seem necessary. We were completely committed to each other and it was only when we began to talk about starting a family that we realised we were both a bit old-fashioned about things like that. So we named the day, 28 April, at the picturesque Norman church of St Mary and St Lawrence in Great Waltham. We had masses of friends from Bolton who we wanted to invite and a whole host of new friends we'd made at Essex, so we looked around but couldn't find anywhere suitable. In the end, we persuaded Richard Bailey (uncle of my Essex team-mate James Foster), the landlord of the Green Man in Great Waltham, the oldest pub in Essex, to let us put up a marquee on his back lawn. We enjoyed a fantastic day with 250 of our friends. I was dressed up in my best bib and tucker, courtesy of Moss Bros, and Lorraine looked breathtakingly stunning.

Things weren't working out so well at Essex. I was still in reasonable form but Paul Prichard was struggling with the captaincy and we never really got our county championship campaign off the ground. The one bright spot was the Benson & Hedges cup. We came second in our group to Middlesex but then beat them narrowly in the quarter-final and made short work of Yorkshire in the semis to book a third successive final at Lord's, this time against Leicestershire. They had a good pace attack that included England pair Chris Lewis and Alan Mullally but we hammered them. Paul Prichard and Nasser Hussain put on a lot of runs and, when Prich was out just short of his century, Nass and I smashed 60 in 11 overs.

Leicestershire were never at the races as Ashley Cowan and Mark Ilott carved their way through them. I have to say that, taken over those three finals, the guy who stands out in my memory is Mark Ilott. He was simply magnificent, bowling left-arm over the wicket from the Pavilion End and using the slope to perfection. In fact, we thought it should be renamed the Ilott End. Mark was in his pomp. He had a big heart and, although he bowled most of his career on flat pitches at Chelmsford, he never stopped trying to make things happen. Conditions at Lord's suited him down to the ground. After Ashley had knocked over the first two Leicestershire batsmen with only six on the board, Mark bowled Phil Simmons with an absolute beauty, pitching on off and swinging back to remove his middle peg. It was an identical ball to the one that had rapped John Crawley on the pad two years before but which somehow David Shepherd saw as not out. I still think we would have won three finals in a row if it hadn't been for that dreadful decision.

Mark was a bit of a character off the pitch but on it he would charge in all day for you. He had a great temperament. There wasn't a lot of love lost between him and Nasser. At times Nass could be really cutting but Mark would just shrug and say, 'That's Nass. That's how he is.' I wish I'd had the opportunity to captain him more but sadly it wasn't to be. He had a really good pain barrier but, being slim, if he picked up an injury it could be a bad one. One day at Southend he got his spikes caught in the turf as he was charging in and went down as though he'd been shot. We all laughed as he dropped like a stone but his cries of pain signalled it was serious. Mark was off for some time and, when he came back, he wasn't the bowler he'd been. It was a worrying situation for him because he was due a benefit season. In order to qualify, he needed to get his contract renewed but there were a few people on the committee who were now reluctant to keep him in the squad.

One of the best things about Nasser is that he firmly believes people should get the rewards they deserve. He and I felt strongly about Mark's situation and had a get-together with Graham Saville before going into the crucial committee meeting to discuss his contract. I had no doubts and said, 'He must be given a new deal and a benefit year. He has sweated blood for this club and, whatever it costs in wages, he has earned a hundred times over. He was one of the key reasons we won good prize money in the last three finals and it was while doing his best for the club that he picked up his injury.'

Nasser and Sav agreed and I was delighted that the whole committee came round to our way of thinking.

People question whether benefit years are still valid these days but I believe they are a good way for the fans to show their appreciation for someone who has given long and loyal service. More importantly, they also provide players with some cash to see them over the difficult period between retiring from cricket and sorting out what they are going to do with the rest of their life.

That meeting was one of the first official functions for the new team of Essex captain Nasser Hussain and his vice captain Ronnie Irani. Despite his man-of-the-match display in the B&H final, Prich had decided to stand down. Winning the cup lost its gloss when we finished rock bottom of the county championship, and it was never clear if Paul jumped or was given an ultimatum. Nasser was the obvious choice to take over. Stuart Law, who had just had his contract extended, was the only other likely candidate but even he acknowledged in an article in the local paper that the job should go to Nass. He also hinted that he would like to be vice captain so clearly he wasn't too happy when I was named. Apparently, he wasn't alone. It turned out that Nasser wasn't keen on me getting the job either.

I only found this out when we had a pre-season training session on Dartmoor, part of which involved Nass, Keith Fletcher, bowling coach Geoff Arnold and I having a private meeting with every player. Robert Rollins was a key member of our squad, a fine wicketkeeper and a solid batsman, capable of getting runs. I believe it was only a bad injury that stopped him becoming England's first black wicketkeeper. He came into his meeting and Nasser's opening remark was: 'Rob, you've got a big season ahead of you. I'll be honest, you were my first choice as vice captain. If I'd had my way, you would have been my man. But don't be too down about it. Keep working on your game and it can be a really big season for you.'

He carried on talking but I didn't take it in because I was

thinking, What the fuck was that all about? I wondered if he'd spoken to Rob during the winter and told him he was getting the job. Anyway, the cat was out of the bag now, so what would Rob's attitude be to me? We already had Stuart Law pissed off, and Prich was still hurting at having to stand down; now he'd provided those two with a possible ally before the season had even started. With Nasser's commitment to England – always his number-one priority – I knew I would be skippering the side most of the season and it was looking likely to be a tricky job. Rob never gave me a moment's trouble but it was an awkward situation that need never have occurred, as Nass admitted when Rob left the room. He said, 'I'm sorry about that, Ronnie. I got that wrong. I shouldn't have said that.'

I was captain for the majority of games during the two years that I was Nasser's number two and it was a steep learning curve for me. I enjoyed the responsibility but wasn't always sure how to handle certain situations and leaned heavily on the advice of John Bird and Frank Dick.

We had a modest season at Essex but I was playing reasonably well and, after some tight bowling against New Zealand at Chelmsford, I was called up for the final Test at the Oval the following week. This was Nasser's first series as England captain. It had been a difficult summer and defeat at the Oval would mean we lost the series 2–1. I didn't realise it at the time but it would be my last Test match.

Nass had said he wanted me in the team because he knew I was a fighter and the kind of player he wanted in the trenches with him. However, by the time they selected the squad to tour South Africa that winter, he and Duncan Fletcher had obviously decided they wanted new blood. A fresh-faced kid called Andrew Flintoff got the spot I was hoping for. I was tossed the consolation prize of an A-team trip and found myself back in New Zealand under the guidance of Mike Gatting. Like Mike Atherton, Gatting was another former England captain who felt he had to live up to the meaning of his Christian name, 'who resembles God'.

I was 28 years old and had been a professional cricketer for ten years but I felt as though my country was telling me I had to start over from scratch. In fact, it was potentially worse than that. Mark Alleyne was given the captaincy, even though his record as an all-rounder wasn't as good as mine, so it was clear he was likely to get the nod ahead of me in the key matches. It appeared I was there to make up the numbers in the less important games and as cover in case Mark picked up an injury.

We had a three-week warm up in Bangladesh and then moved on to New Zealand. I never felt that my input was welcome by the management so I tended to do my work and keep out of the way. In the past, I'd done extra training to try to impress the selectors but it had never worked, so when we were given some time off in Christchurch I decided to go fishing. I was picked up at 5.30am and taken to Lake Shepherd, which has a stream running into it that is so pure my guide just scooped out a cupful of water and said, 'Try that – you'll never taste anything better.' It was stunning and made a fabulous brew of tea. I caught a lot of brown trout and we also shot a wild pig. We took them back to the hotel and the chef cooked up a feast – fish with Thai sauce followed by roast pig. The lads loved it.

I didn't think there could be a more attractive fishing spot – until the following week when he took me out of town in the opposite direction. As we drove along, I saw a pinhead of turquoise in the distance and slowly it got bigger. This was

Lake Coleridge. It was breathtakingly beautiful and we stood on crystal rock in the water, spinning for trout. Paradise.

The downside of Christchurch was that I caught chickenpox. Young Michael Gough, a talented prospect from Durham who was on his first tour, also went down with it and the two of us were quarantined from the rest of the squad. They then moved off to Wellington, leaving us in the hotel. At first the chickenpox was horrendous. I felt listless and itchy as hell but then the symptoms seem to ease up. However, the doctor wouldn't release us to join up with the rest of the squad for a few more days. Michael and I hit it off and spent a lot of time talking cricket. We also had a couple of nights in the bar. We received a daily phone call from the physio, Anne, and one day she said, 'You sound dreadful, Ronnie. Take care of yourself.' Little did she realise that we'd only just got in from the night before.

Eventually, we were released and joined the rest of the party a few days before the first match against New Zealand A. It was only when I started training again that I realised just how much the chickenpox had taken out of me. As soon as I did any sustained exercise, I felt knackered, which was quite alarming because I've always prided myself on my stamina and ability to keep going no matter how gruelling it gets. Now I was putting in a bowling session in the morning and going back to my room for an hour's sleep to recover.

As expected, Mark Alleyne filled the all-rounder spot to play New Zealand A. I joined in the nets and fielding practice with the team in the morning and again in the gym sessions in the evening, but in between I would often catch some kip in the dressing room. That apparently didn't go down well with the management. As soon as the match was over, I was summoned to a meeting with Mike Gatting,

Martyn Moxon, who was acting as coach on the trip, and Mark Alleyne.

Gatting didn't bother with pleasantries. 'We've got a serious issue here,' he said.

My heart sank. Not again, I thought. I wondered if Michael Gough had let slip that we'd had a couple of nights on the bevvies in Christchurch or maybe the hotel had said something, although we'd never caused any trouble.

'We take it very seriously and I've already spoken to Lord McLaurin and David Graveney at the ECB.'

It looked as though, whatever it was I was accused of, I'd been found guilty before the trial had even been called. I said, 'What exactly is the problem?'

'We feel that you weren't putting in enough effort in the warm-up this morning. In fact, we've not been impressed with you since you came back from Christchurch. You've not been mixing as we think you should and for the last two nights in the gym, especially last night, you didn't work as hard as you should on the bikes and the cross-trainers. Can you explain your actions, because at the moment we are thinking of sending you home?'

If Gatting had hoped to intimidate me, he'd failed. As I listened to him, I sensed that he was trying to make an impression, to show the ECB how tough he could be as a team manager on tour. I was the ideal target. I'd had problems before and I was quite senior so he couldn't be accused of picking on one of the youngsters. It seemed a bit rich to be threatened with public humiliation for failing to pedal a bike hard enough by a man who as captain of England had brought a Test match to a grinding halt when he went nose to nose with umpire Shakoor Rana and later had to apologise for his foul language. At that stage, I felt as though I had nothing to lose, so I decided to say what I thought.

'Is that it?' I asked.

'Yes. What have you got to say?'

'You are fucking joking, aren't you?'

'No. I don't think you realise how serious this is.'

'Is that right? I have just spent ten days with chickenpox which has knocked the stuffing out of me and at times I'm still knackered. Nevertheless, I've joined in with everything you have asked me to do and, as to mixing, I've always helped and encouraged the young players but I didn't want to cut across what Mark was doing. Now you are threatening to send me home because you don't think I rode a fucking bike hard enough and didn't put enough effort into the warm-up for a match I wasn't playing in?'

Gatting tried to interrupt, saying, 'Those fielding drills are important.'

I was seething by this stage and cut across him. 'Shut up, Mike. You've had your say. I've been playing cricket professionally for ten years – of course I know how important fielding drills are and I played my part fully. I respected you as a cricketer and thought you were a fine captain of England but I have to say you've gone right down in my estimation today. And don't bother to send me home, I'll buy my own ticket because this is just a fucking farce.'

'There's no need to be like that.'

'No need? You bring me in here to threaten me over something that could have been handled with a quiet word. You tell me you've contacted the chairman of the ECB and the chairman of selectors about me, before you've heard my side of things. And all because you don't think I rode a bike the way you think I should. Martyn, you've been working with me all through the tour. Have I ever flunked a moment's work?'

Martyn Moxon looked uncomfortable and Gatting was red-faced. I don't think he had expected me to come back at him.

Mark Alleyne spoke up for the first time: 'Look, guys, maybe this has got blown out of proportion. Let's regroup and get on with the tour.'

As soon as I got out of the room, I went and found Michael Gough and told him what had happened. I said, 'You are just making your way at this level so make sure you don't give them any reason to pull you up. Put in even more effort, so they can't say anything to you.'

Once again, any pleasure I got out of touring for my country had been destroyed by a management who wanted everyone to conform to their notion of what was right. I have always prided myself on being a team player, always gone out of my way to back my captain, to encourage young players and be supportive to those who are having a bad time either personally or from lack of form. I was being tagged as the bad boy of the party once again. It was so disheartening that my future as an England player always seemed to be in the hands of those who didn't appreciate me.

Gradually my energy levels came back and I played in one or two of the ODIs and did quite well, putting on some runs with a promising-looking batsman called Marcus Trescothick. He was one of the finds of the tour and, when I got back and Nasser asked me who had impressed me, I immediately said, 'Trescothick. He's the best batsman in the country at the moment and could do a job for England. He's a top left-hander, got all the strokes, loads of time, a great temperament and is a good gripper in the slips as well.'

'Are we still talking about Trescothick or are we on Bradman now?' Nasser mocked.

'I'm telling you, he's the real deal. The other guy who's ready is David Sales of Northampton.'

'We like lardy cricketers, do we?' Nass grinned.

'He's a big lad but he's athletic and, make no mistake, he can bat.'

Nasser was still sceptical but I understand that, when he mentioned Tres's name a few weeks later, Duncan Fletcher agreed with me, so Nass came on board and Marcus went on to play 76 Tests and 123 ODIs.

I finished the New Zealand tour in good form, so, when Andrew Flintoff picked up an injury in South Africa, I thought I might get a call-up to replace him but instead they sent Craig White. They'd already included that joker Gavin Hamilton from Yorkshire, a player who chirped so much I always thought he must live on bird seed, so I concluded my England career was over. The injustice of it burned me up. I decided to ring David Graveney and ask him why I'd been overlooked. I'd always got on well with Grav. I'd played against him when he was at Durham. He was good company and a decent bloke. Everyone thinks they know better than the chairman of selectors, but I thought on the whole he did a good job and felt the press treated him unfairly.

After the usual pleasantries, I got to the point of the call: 'Grav, don't take this the wrong way but I need to know something. I had a good season at Essex, was first-choice all-rounder for the final Test at the Oval and went on the A tour where I did really well once I'd recovered from chickenpox. I realise why Andrew Flintoff got the nod ahead of me but I can't work out why I wasn't called up once he was injured. What's that all about?'

'I understand what you're saying, Ronnie. But you got a poor tour report from New Zealand. Mike Gatting said you were a bad influence on the young players. And you do have form on this. You are not considered a good tourist.'

'Grav, that's a joke. Is that why I wasn't picked?'

'It certainly didn't help your cause. I have to say I was surprised when I read the report because you've always been fine when I've been around you and I like the way you play your cricket, but they are the management and I have to go by what they say.'

'Grav, I'm shattered. I've always been a team player and I work for the team to do well even if I'm not playing. Gatting's criticisms in New Zealand were a joke and the stuff before that was bullshit. David Lloyd was wrong when he accused me of going on tour injured and the mooning incident wasn't anything to do with me. So how come I'm a bad tourist?'

'Sorry, Ronnie. But I can only go by what I'm told.'

I felt sick. It all seemed so unjust. But I was determined they wouldn't drag me down again. I would prove them wrong by doing even better at Essex.

CHAPTER 17
YOU SHOULD INVEST IN DOT.COM

One of the best decisions Lorraine and I ever made was to buy the first addition to our family. He weighed in at nine stones and Eric the Doberman was a massive bonus at a bleak time in our lives.

The new millennium arrived in a frenzy of optimism around the world but Lorraine and I had been through a horrendous spell. She had twice suffered the trauma of miscarriage, which was heart-breaking for me but much worse for her, especially as I wasn't able to be around as much as I should have been because I was trying to sort out the problems in my career. We both wanted children badly but began to fear it would never happen.

Sadness like that is not the kind of thing you can share with blokes in a dressing room. And, no matter how much you love each other, it's sometimes easier for a husband and wife to keep their fears to themselves in case you hurt the other person. I think it must be very hard to be a woman and I know that, like most men, there have been many occasions when I haven't really grasped what my wife was going through. As a man, you want to help and to be a comfort but it's not always easy to know when to be strong and when to be soft, when to let them sort things out for themselves because that's what they want to do, or when to try to take the problem away. I know I have made things worse by trying to do what I thought was right and there have been times when I should have put my career on the back burner for a few days and spent the time with my family.

Eric turned out to be something of a lifeline for both of us. He provided Lorraine with company and comfort when I was away and I just loved the fact that, whenever I came home, his silly little stumpy tail would wag (they were still docked in those days). I would take him running and he always cheered me up. Almost as soon as we got Eric, Lorraine became pregnant again. I'll let her tell you the full story in a later chapter, but I am convinced that Eric's arrival played a part in that.

A lot of people have the wrong idea about Dobermans. Because they are so big, people assume they are aggressive but I think dogs reflect the temperament of their owners. Eric and our latest acquisition Zara (a Doberman pup) are great about the house, terrific with the children and would only act threateningly if I ordered them to in some kind of emergency. I was particularly chuffed when I met former Leeds United footballer Gary Speed on *A Question of Sport*, and he told me Eric Cantona had a Doberman. I knew that man had taste!

I had a bee in my bonnet that I wanted to move house, or rather I wanted to find somewhere I could build my dream house. At first Lorraine thought I was nuts. As she said, we were living in a gorgeous cottage in Great Waltham, one of the nicest villages in Essex, so why would we want to move? Her doubts increased tenfold when I showed her what I was planning to buy – an unprepossessing 1940s house down a lane in Felsted. It was another charming village but the house wasn't a patch on the one we were already living in. It had no central heating, mice in the attic and had become too much for the elderly couple who lived there and so was rather rundown. But I had got to know a local builder and seen what he could do, and I thought he might just be able to turn this plot into something that we could have only dreamed of when we were growing up in Bolton.

I'd met Nick Bones a few years before and we'd done a couple of deals together, including buying a pub that he had converted into two terrific cottages. If I could get my sums right, I reckoned we could knock down the 1940s house and Nick would build us a really special home on the site.

I needed to get a price on our place in Great Waltham and the first assessment wasn't encouraging. The estate agent reckoned he could get £195,000 but I'd been looking at a lot of houses by this stage and thought his estimate was low – certainly too low to allow me to do what I wanted to do. I had a word with the guy who was selling the house in Felsted. He was much more upbeat and managed to get an offer for £250,000 on the table within three days. We then managed to negotiate the price on the Felsted property down to £265,000. So far the figures added up. But then there was the small matter of cash to demolish the existing place and build the new one. I reckoned the total cost was something over half a million and I would need an initial mortgage of £80,000 to get things under way. Time to call on an old friend.

Alan Leach had been my accountant since the days of the fruit and veg shop in Bolton. I'd played junior football with his son Andrew, and after the match Alan was the guy you always wanted to get a lift from because he had the best car, an Opel Monza, and he would take you to the shop and buy everyone a Mars bar and a can of pop. I went to his office in Horwich and we fixed the mortgage. As I was signing the papers, the lady who worked for him said, 'Take good care of this money, Ronnie, because they won't release any more until they've seen what you've done with it. The next lot of cash will depend on the value of what you've built with this lot.'

'Don't worry,' I joked. 'I'll put it in stocks and shares until I need it.'

She went pale. 'Whatever you do, don't do that. It's far too risky.'

I assured her I was joking and with the cash in place set about applying for planning permission. The architect advised me to ask for much more than I wanted on the grounds that planning committees usually reject the first application on big projects. 'Then you can apply for what you really want and you will almost certainly get it,' he said.

It seemed logical, so we put in an application for two houses on the plot and duly got knocked back. Just in case we got another negative decision, the second application was for a single house, much bigger than we wanted and costing a lot more to build, and sod's law they accepted it. Suddenly I needed more cash.

I approached another adviser I had been using in London and he suggested I should put some money into the shares of a company called Affinity Internet Services, one of the fastest-growing dot.com companies and a sure thing. I took his advice and, ignoring that warning voice at the back of my head, bought a thousand shares at £60 each out of my first mortgage money. Within a few weeks the shares were worth

£80 each, I'd made 20 grand profit and decided to sell. But my adviser urged me to stay in. 'They will go to £120,' he said. 'I'm negotiating to get some more.'

I didn't buy any more but I didn't sell, and the next few weeks were like a long, drawn-out nightmare in which I was trapped in an ever more horrendous car crash. Each day as I looked in the newspaper, the shares slipped back. They were soon down to £60 again, then £40. I was panicking but the adviser assured me they would bounce back. They never did and very soon they were down to £5 and unsellable. In effect, they were worth nothing at all.

While all this was going on, I was grappling with being the new captain of Essex in a period when all kinds of things were starting to bubble under the surface, mainly involving Stuart Law. At times it was only Eric's little tail wagging that kept me going.

It was clear that, with Nasser's England commitments, he couldn't continue to captain Essex and Graham Saville asked me to take over. I was thrilled. The county was going through a transition period and there were a few rumbles in the dressing room, but I was up for the challenge. I was proud to be asked, even though I knew I'd have more problems from Stuart Law.

Stuart was one of the finest batsmen I ever shared a stand with. He had a typical Australian attitude to sport: tough, no quarter asked or given, always determined to win, and then, as soon as play was over, off to unwind with a beer. With his ability to score runs, you have to ask yourself why he only played one Test match for his country. He was certainly talented enough. The only reason I can come up with is that the Aussie selectors weighed up his character and decided they didn't want him in the dressing room.

At times he could be terrific company and, as I've said, a match-winner. He was great to bat with. Unlike someone like Nasser, who completely concentrated on his own innings, Stuart was willing to talk and encourage the guy at the other end. Yet, whenever I think of him, I'm reminded of the story of the scorpion on the camel's back. The tale goes that they are both in the desert and the scorpion is desperate for water. The camel gives it a ride to a water hole and, as it bends down to let the scorpion get to the water, it gives the camel a poisonous bite. 'Why did you do that?' asks the camel. 'I carried you across the desert to find water.' The scorpion replies, 'I don't know. It's just in my nature.'

Stuart had an uncanny ability to hurt his friends. Paul Prichard was supposed to be his big mate at Essex yet, when there was a discussion about what was going wrong, Stuart said: 'We know who the problem is. I travel with him every day.'

Stuart was never a big supporter of Nasser and I was aware in my time as vice captain – and now as captain – that he was encouraging a certain amount of dissent. I suspect it was mainly because he felt he should have had the job. He'd been a successful club captain in Australia and had skippered the Australian U19 side. But I also think it was just in his nature.

It's quite easy to undermine a captain if you want to. There are always people who are out of the side or don't think they are getting enough bowling or batting high enough up the order, and are there to be picked off. If you are not careful, splits can occur, which is very unhealthy. It's not important for everyone to get on as best buddies in a dressing room – there are too many different characters for that – but you should be united in wanting the group to do well.

The 2000 season was the first after the county

championship had been split into two divisions and Essex were in Division Two. I've never been a big fan of dividing the competition. I can see that it adds a bit of excitement with promotion and relegation but one of the key points of the county game is to prepare players for Test cricket, yet under this system you are condemning half the players to never playing against some of the top internationals who are in the other division. And the English weather can make winning and losing such a lottery that you can find good sides relegated because they've been unlucky with the rain one summer.

Still, if there is a prize to be won, I'm always up to try to win it and my first season as captain saw Essex in contention for promotion despite losing a number of matches to a miserable summer. In the end, it came down to the last session of the final match and a bit of kidology on my part.

Going into the match against Warwickshire at Chelmsford, we were in the third and final promotion spot. Our opponents were one place behind us and two or three other clubs also had a chance of overtaking us, especially Nottinghamshire and Gloucestershire who were playing each other at Bristol. A draw and bonus points might be enough for us, but I was aware that the other two would do everything in their power to make sure they got a result and the winner could just pip us.

Warwickshire tore us apart on the first day. Their opening pair, Mark Wagh and Michael Powell, each hit centuries and put on 230 for the first wicket. On day two, they reached 400-8 and their captain Neil Smith cleverly declared, giving them maximum batting bonus points while denying us extra bowling points. Our strategy was changing. Our first priority now was to reach the 251 we needed to avoid the follow-on.

Before long we were 63-3 with Paul Prichard, Paul Grayson and Stuart Law back in the pavilion. I went in with Darren Robinson and he played a superb innings, just missing out on his century. By the close of play, I was unbeaten on 72 and we still needed 43 to reach our target.

I spent much of Thursday night tossing and turning, going over the figures in my head, trying to work out the best way to handle things – and wishing I'd paid more attention in maths class at school. When I got to the ground on Friday morning, it was raining hard and no play looked likely, which changed everything again. It put pressure on Warwickshire, who definitely needed a win. I realised that Neil Smith was in the market for a deal that would give them a chance of victory and decided it was time to use some of the negotiating skills Fil Mercer had taught me in the fruit and veg market.

Sky were covering the match and, when Ian Botham interviewed Neil and me to fill some of the time as the rain poured down, I made it clear that I thought all Essex had to do was to keep on batting until we reached 350. That would give us three batting points and, with the four for a draw, I confidently predicted we would go up. Deep down, I felt we needed to win to be certain but I could see that my apparent confidence was swaying Neil towards offering more than he wanted. We had a couple of chats during the day and I kept repeating that, while I was happy to try to make a game of it, we still felt that we could bat it out.

The final day loomed and it was still raining. Neil was desperately keen to reach a compromise and agreed that, if we declared where we were, they would set us a reasonable target. That was just what I'd been hoping for, but I said I'd have to think it over, pointing out that the wicket was much tougher to bat on now and would give their attack all the aces. We knew from Ceefax that Gloucestershire and Nottinghamshire were playing and likely to get a result, so we were now both desperate to get our game on. It was half past one before the umpires decided it was fit to play. I declared at our overnight score, Warwickshire hit eight runs off three balls and then declared, leaving us to chase 201 and themselves 56 overs to get us out. It was a generous declaration and our dressing room thought we just needed the weather to hold for us to win. By tea, we were 64-4 and struggling.

It was now down to me and Stephen Peters, a youngster finding it hard to live up to his junior promise which had seen him score a century for Essex at 17 and be a star player for England U19s. He was taking time to adapt to first-class cricket and made a shaky start to his innings but I kept talking to him and gradually he blossomed and played one of the best knocks of his career. It was the kind of situation I've always relished and, despite playing in light rain, he and I got on top of the attack. I thumped one of Graham Gooch's favourite straight drives to the boundary to clinch victory with 17 overs to spare. We had secured second place in the table and won promotion. It was time to uncork the champagne and celebrate my first success as a captain.

Just over a week later, on 25 September, the bubbly was out again, celebrating the birth of our first daughter. Being a modern man, I attended all the ante-natal classes. I wasn't impressed with the breathing exercises, but, as an only child who was completely unused to being around small people, the training on how to hold a baby, how to bath it and, most importantly, how to change a nappy was invaluable.

Lorraine bloomed in pregnancy. She enjoyed it and carried it off with style. And yes, I was there helping when she gave birth in St John's Hospital in Chelmsford. She was determined not to have an epidural and, over the ten-hour labour, the gas and air didn't always seem to do the trick when the going got really tough, so at one stage she sank her teeth into me. A little later, a male nurse, with his deep insight into what it's like for a woman to have a baby, walked by and flippantly said, 'Have the injection, dear – it's not a bravery contest, you know.' He was lucky Lorraine was in no condition to move or he would have received much more than a dirty look.

Finally, our first daughter was born. The main thing I remember is thinking how gorgeous she looked and what wonderful eyelashes she had. In the weeks leading up to the birth, we'd been round the houses trying to come up with a name, but in the end we decided on Simone Patricia Anne. Simone was the name of the midwife who delivered her and we both really liked it. The other two names were after Lorraine's mum and my mum.

Simone was premature so she took a lot of looking after. She cried a lot at night with colic and it wasn't long before Lorraine and I were both knackered. I'm the first to admit it's much harder for women – babies completely depend on their mum – so I can only imagine what it was like for Lorraine having to feed her every four hours, 24/7. I had it easy by comparison and still felt exhausted. Fortunately, since training for kick boxing as a kid, I've developed a kind of addiction to endurance – I get to the stage where just keeping going gives me a buzz, and that took over as we saw Simone through her first few weeks.

We were still trying to sort out the hassles over building our new house so we had moved into the 1940s place, which tended to be drafty and chilly. There were many nights I would pick Simone up when she was crying, lay her on my chest and pull the covers over us. My heartbeat seemed to send her off to sleep. It was a wonderful feeling. I was an immensely proud dad and would take her in her carrycot to the cricket ground while I had meetings about the upcoming season. And I was obsessive about her having a dry nappy – I'd often change her when there was no need at all.

She also gave me a new incentive to sort out the financial problems on the house to provide her with somewhere she could grow up warm and secure.

CHAPTER 18

LEAVE ENOUGH GAP
TO CREATE A SPARK

The dream house was turning into a nightmare. Instead of foundations, it felt as though we were digging a huge hole into which I was chucking money. At times it felt as though my best hope of getting it built was if we struck oil. I'd paid a heavy price to learn that dabbling in the stock market is not for those who know sod all about it and don't have time to learn. I was stretched to the limit financially. The estimate for building the house had gone up by £100,000 and when Nick took a close look at the land he found it needed piling to strengthen it, which cost another £28,000. We had to move out of the old house so we could pull it down and found a place across the road to rent but that was setting me back £750 a month. Everything I was earning at Essex was going straight back out each month and the money I'd saved from playing for England was now being ploughed into the first stage of building.

I had always planned to have a triple garage with a large granny flat over the top and I decided we would start with that, reckoning that once it was built we could move into the flat and save ourselves the house rent. Bad move. We got it put up but, when we called in the surveyor from the Bradford & Bingley to give the go-ahead to release the next block of money, he knocked us back. He claimed the garage/flat had no value without the house and he needed to see progress in that direction before he could release more cash.

'But I've spent 80 grand,' I protested. 'I need that money.'

'Sorry, there's nothing I can do. No one is going to buy a flat above a garage. It's worthless as it stands. Call me when you've made a start on the house.'

I was fucked. I dared not tell him I was out of money or he might pull the plug altogether. I needed a Plan B. I just couldn't think of one.

After several sleepless nights, I persuaded myself that I could sort it out in the long term. I had a benefit coming up in the next couple of years and that would put things back on an even keel. I tried to be my usual bouncy self around the cricket club – I didn't want them to know what a prat I'd been with the mortgage money – but to be honest my mind was frazzled, which is why when Nancy Fuller asked me to go to a charity function I turned her down. Nancy is another of those superb people who do so much behind the scenes to make things work smoothly, so I felt bad about saying no. She looked a bit surprised because I'd always been happy to go on personal appearances at schools or charity dos. In fact, I quite liked them.

'OK, Ronnie,' she said, 'but they will be ever so disappointed. They specifically said they wanted you because you would be able to raise the most money.'

I knew I should go and said, 'All right. What is it again?'

Nancy explained it was called Jail Break and that I would be locked up in Chelmsford prison for the day until enough of my friends agreed to pay money to the charity to get me out. Ah well, I thought wryly, at least I'll have a roof over my head and three meals a day.

That's how I found myself sitting in a cold cell chatting to a guy with a Caribbean accent who was also part of the Jail Break scheme. He told me his name was Damian Thompson. He was great company, loved his cricket and we talked about the game for ages. I finally said, 'And what about you? What do you do?'

'I'm the manager of the local Halifax Building Society.'

I laughed.

'What's so funny?'

I felt it would be inappropriate to burden him with my problems so just said, 'Nothing. I'm building my own house at the moment and there are a few problems. I might need a good building society.'

'Here's my card. Just give me a call. Whatever it is you need, I'm sure we can help.'

I thought, You don't know what you're saying, pal.

We shook hands when we parted and a few days later I decided there was nothing to lose in talking to him. With Simone still suffering with colic, there was no way I could move her and Lorraine into a flat on a noisy, dirty building site. I needed to take some decisive action.

I decided I had to put all my cards on the table so, when I saw Damian, I went through all the figures, not keeping anything back. At the end of it, I said, 'Can you help me?'

He didn't commit himself but immediately arranged for an independent surveyor to visit the site and a few days later called me up: 'Good news, Ronnie. Based on the figures you've given me of your earnings and the valuation of the property, you can borrow at least another £150,000 without a problem.'

It was as though someone had thrown me a lifeline just as I was going down for the third time. It was only then that I realised just how much it had been wearing me down. I rang Nick and gave him the good news.

Gradually, the house was built and it was everything we could have asked for. The family even surprised me by arranging for a set of stumps and a cricket ball to be built in the stair rail that leads up from the hall.

Soon after we moved in, Nasser dropped me off at home following one of his rare days playing for Essex. He'd last seen the place when the old house was on the site and had told me he thought I was a complete idiot for buying it. I tried to explain my vision for what it could become but he just said, 'You're stark raving mad to leave that nice house at Great Waltham for this. I'm telling you, you've had a mare.' He hadn't been near since, so he didn't know about all the work that had gone on. He pulled into the driveway and to my surprise jumped out of the car. I thought he was going to get my bag out of the boot but he just walked straight into the house.

When I joined him in the hall, which is quite impressive if I say so myself, he was just staring around. Finally, he said, 'How the fuck can a couple from Bolton afford a place like this?'

I thought, Cheeky sod, but just smiled and said, 'Vision, mate. That's all you need. Vision.'

But things were not going well at Essex. We had a lot of young players who were struggling to come to terms with life in the top flight and Stuart Law was being even more disruptive. He let little things niggle him, like the fact that Nasser had a better car than he did. I tried to point out that Nass was captain of England so he was bound to have top of the range, but he couldn't see it. It was sad that he felt so disillusioned and I knew that behind my back he was plotting to get me out. He started to court a few of the members to his cause and I wondered if I should do anything.

Amid all this I had a worrying time over Dad. He'd started to complain that he was getting out of breath walking up the hills to Old Trafford. When I pointed out there weren't any hills, he brushed it off and said, 'Must be the onions in the burgers disagreeing with me. I've been to see the doctor and he says I'm OK.'

I still wasn't happy and, after taking a lot of expert advice, I took Dad to see Dr Clesham, a top consultant who did an angiogram and said that Dad needed a new heart valve and double bypass. Dad loved a drop of scotch and soda, so it wasn't easy when he was asked to choose between a metal valve which would require him to take warfarin for the rest of his life and give up alcohol, or a pig's valve, which would probably need to be replaced every ten years. After several meetings with top heart surgeon Kit Wong, Dad eventually plumped for the metal valve and went into hospital in London to have the op.

Visiting him that day was scary. My strong dad, a man who had always enjoyed such good health and been so active, was lying there with tubes coming out of him and looking frightened. He gradually got his strength back and is still in Bolton, not as mobile as he used to be, but still taking me to task if he thinks I'm going wrong. Sometime after the operation he queried why I had got out in the 90s for about the third innings running. 'You must go on and make the hundred,' he said.

'I'm doing it for you, Dad,' I said.

'What do you mean? I don't want you to get out.'

'No, but you always used to have a large Jamesons when I scored a hundred and I can't take that risk!'

As well as coping with all that, I was trying to improve things for the club and the players by getting involved in fundraising. I thought it was important that we travelled as a team, so I was particularly keen for the club to buy a team bus to take us to matches rather than driving around in our cars. I worked closely with Alan Lilley, the cricket operations manager at the club, and we invented all kinds of packages that people could buy into. I remember visiting loads of companies as diverse as Broad Oak Farm Sausages, Mid Essex Gravel and Geoff Aslett's tunnelling company Molegrove and persuading them to become involved in the club. It was hard work but I felt it was important. Cash was short and, if we weren't careful, that would affect the performance on the pitch. At one stage, it looked as though we might have to cut our bowling coach Geoff Arnold to reduce the wages budget. That would have been disastrous, so Keith Fletcher and I went out and raised the money to hang on to him.

I didn't mind the work – it was still easier than getting up at 2am to buy spuds on a freezing morning in Manchester – but I'll admit there were times when I felt out of my depth and I spent hours on the phone to John Bird and Frank Dick asking what I should do. Frank suggested I was taking too much on myself and should just concentrate on affecting what went on out on the pitch and leave some of the other stuff to the club officials.

He also gave me one terrific image of captaincy that has stuck with me and which helped enormously as things started to blow up around me. He said, 'Ronnie, they are your team-mates and they know you well. They know you are someone who enjoys the social side as well as the cricket so, if you try to change completely, they will suss out you are being false.

On the other hand, you can no longer be one of the boys. It's a fine line. The best way to think about it is like a spark plug – if the distance is too great the spark can't get across and if it's too close it is snuffed out. You have to try to find exactly the right gap to get the spark going.'

I felt sure I still had the support of the key people at Essex, people like Doug Insole, Keith Fletcher, Graham Gooch, Graham Saville and David Ackfield. They all knew the game inside out and had spotted what was going on with Stuart. I decided just to get on with the job of doing my best for the team. If it was decided the captaincy should be taken away from me, so be it – all I could do was give 100 per cent. I've always believed that the club and badge are more important than any individual, including me.

Things came to a head when Nass did an interview with Simon Hughes for the *Daily Telegraph*. I'm sure he meant no malice but in explaining how people approach the game in different ways he said something along the lines of 'Some work hard, are totally focused and get an early night so they are ready for play the following day, while others like to go out for a few drinks like Stuart Law and Paul Prichard.'

Stuart immediately photocopied the piece and left copies lying around the dressing room. I thought Nasser had made a mistake but didn't want to condemn him when he wasn't there, even though I was left to deal with disgruntled players saying, 'I can't believe Nass has done that.' I could sense the lads were sympathising with Stuart over this and maybe starting to take his side in some of his other complaints.

Nass happened to see a copy of the article on our dressing-room bench, realised what was happening and lost his cool. He demanded a meeting with the chief executive David East, Keith Fletcher, Sav, me, Stuart Law and Paul Prichard. We'd hardly sat down when he tore into Prich. 'I'm sick and tired of this back-stabbing. Prich. I've known you since you were a kid. How can you turn on me like this?'

To his credit, Paul kept his temper. He just said, 'Read the article, Nass. You made it look as though I'm unprofessional. What do you expect?'

Nass wouldn't have that and insisted on an immediate meeting with all the players and, as soon as everyone was assembled, he started to rant at them. 'I'm sick of you lot and your back-stabbing. You used to be my team but you're not my boys any more. The England lads are my boys now. I'm done here.' And with that he stormed out.

We limped through the rest of the season a pretty unhappy bunch and it was no real surprise when we were relegated. Something drastic had to be done and the committee decided that Stuart Law had to go. No matter how prolific and talented he was as a batsman, the price in the dressing room was too high. I tried to talk to Stuart before he left and asked him why it had come to this. He and I had shared some great times at the wicket but now it had all turned sour. I said, 'What's your problem?'

'The Essex fans don't want you,' he replied. 'They want me.'

'That's not for us to decide. That's up to the committee and they've made their decision.'

I had a chat with Keith Fletcher and he said, 'Don't worry, Ronnie. We are all behind you. The fans may be unhappy for a while at losing a player of Stuart's ability but they don't know the whole story. You are doing well as captain. I'm sure most of the supporters are on your side.'

Once again, Fletch turned out to be right on the button. The 2002 season turned out to be one of the biggest of my career.

CHAPTER 19

YOU'RE THE MAN TO TAKE SACHIN

The year got off to a perfect start when I found myself back at St John's Hospital in Chelmsford on 6 January, rubbing soothing oils into Lorraine's back as she gave birth to our second daughter, Maria Jane. It had been another super pregnancy – I had chosen my breeding stock well! – and it was helped by the fact that Lorraine's mum Pat had moved in with us and become part of the family. I even managed to persuade Lorraine to stop pushing long enough for me to see the end of Manchester United beating West Ham in the FA Cup on TV. Maria was born in injury time. Her arrival meant another bout of sleepless nights and a lot of shoving food through the blender – Lorraine insisted on all natural food – but she was worth it.

Things were also getting exciting on the cricket front. Before the season had even started, I knew it was going to be a lot better. Stuart Law had moved on to Lancashire and, even more important, Graham Gooch was going to be more hands-on as the team coach. His first decision turned out to be a gem – he brought in Andy Flower as our new overseas player. Andy was sheer class. At that time he was one of the top-rated batsmen in Test cricket, which was some feat when you consider he was never able to face his own Zimbabwe bowlers. He was also one of the finest wicketkeepers in the world and turned out to be a great influence in the dressing room. He was completely supportive, always positive and ever ready to help the young players. The atmosphere at the club was transformed. He made the job of being captain so much easier.

Working on a daily basis with Goochie and sharing the crease with Andy, my batting went up to another level. Andy and I scored a lot of runs together. It was a great combination – a right- and left-hander so the bowlers could never get set; he would manipulate the bowling and make them defensive so I could be aggressive. And we talked a lot, keeping each other going out there. I am not at all surprised that Andy has gone on to become a top coach and landed the England job. I think he will do terrifically well and to my mind the dream ticket would now be to bring in Graham Gooch as the England team manager.

I have been very fortunate and played with some great wicketkeepers in my career but Andy's presence behind the stumps also improved my bowling. James Foster had kept for us but he was off at university. James probably had the best hands of the lot and that is saying something when you consider I've played alongside Alec Stewart, Jack Russell, Keith Piper and Warren Hegg. It's a travesty that James has only played a handful of Tests for England but, having got the nod, he suffered a freak accident in the nets at Chelmsford when a ball from Andy Clark smashed his arm and, by the time he was fit again, Alec Stewart was firmly entrenched once more. Fozzy could bat a bit as well. He was

Nasser Hussain congratulates me on reaching my half-century in that never-to-be-forgotten match at the Oval in July 2002.

Time to celebrate! Indian batsman Dinesh Mongia caught off my bowling by Alex Stewart during the NatWest series final at Lord's in July 2002.

Above: Proud Essex captain: two titles that season.   © *Kieran Galvin*

Below: Celebrating winning the Totes league title. Essex v Worcestershire in
September 2005.

Another great Twenty20 night at Chelmsford, another Irani six against Hampshire!

© *Kieran Galvin*

Above: Last game of the season. I save Essex from relegation with a 'daddy' hundred against Glamorgan.
© *Kieran Galvin*

Below: Working up the crowd during England's one-day international against Australia in December 2002.
© *Getty Images*

Above: Me helping Ravi Bopara to work on his bowling and the art of reverse swing. He can do a job for England used the right way.

Right: Ryan ten Doeschate congratulates me on the double century as we just miss out on a record partnership.

© Kieran Galvin

Above: My final walk around the county ground at Chelmsford, thanking the Essex fans for their support. My boys give me the guard of honour send off!

Below left: On the pavilion steps for the last time as a player with my two favourite Essex girls.

Below right: A moment I'll never forget.

© Kieran Galvin

Above: With Jamie Redknapp, who is a great mate.

Middle: On the mic.

Below: The talkSPORT line-up

a dogged terrier of a batsman who would knuckle down and dig out the runs, especially in one-day cricket and was greatly appreciated by his team-mates. We also had a fine keeper in Barry Hyam, who had two of the best hands I've come across. I've seen him win man-of-the-match awards just for his keeping, pulling off some incredible catches. But sadly he struggled to make an impact with the bat, and you need runs from your keeper.

Having Andy Flower behind the stumps changed things for me because he was willing to stand up to the wicket. Every other keeper I'd played with stood back but now batsmen were unable to come down the wicket to me and try to knock me off a length and I started to pick up more and more wickets.

I was producing some of the best cricket of my life and, while I'd always enjoyed playing, even in the bad times, this was better than anything I'd experienced since I was a kid. Essex were winning matches and on course to reclaim their place in Division One and the media were floating my name to play for England again.

I was desperate for another chance to pull on an England sweater once more, especially with the World Cup coming up the following winter, but hardly dared hope I would get a recall. I tried not to get my hopes up too high but I'd never lost belief that I was good enough and just hoped that the selectors were noticing what was happening at Chelmsford. It turned out they were. When the squad was announced for the triangular NatWest ODI tournament with Sri Lanka and India, I was in. All I had to do was to reproduce my county form at international level and I might be able to book a seat on the World Cup plane.

England started with a victory over Sri Lanka at Trent

Bridge where Stewie and I put on a rapid 95 before Freddie Flintoff smashed the fastest ever half-century by an England player, 50 off 18 balls. The second match was against India at Lord's and as usual Duncan Fletcher was his meticulous self, sitting us down to watch videos of the opposition and discuss how we would handle each of them. At the time Sachin Tendulkar was in his prime. The 'little master' was scoring runs for fun and bowlers were despairing about where to put the ball to him. You seldom felt you could tempt him into anything even slightly rash. With someone like Brian Lara, who I'm proud to say I once dismissed in both innings of a match against Warwickshire, you always felt you had a chance because you could bowl a good line and length and he would still risk an edge or miss-hit trying to smash you out of the ground. But Tendulkar would respect a good ball and only when you strayed, even slightly, would he take you on. It would usually result in a four or a six, so you can imagine everyone's reaction when my mate Darren Gough said, 'You're the man for Tendulkar, Ronnie.'

As the laughter died down, I grinned and said, 'Don't take the piss, Goughie.'

'No, I'm serious. He won't like batting against you. He doesn't like your type of bowling.'

'What? Crap?'

Darren smiled. 'No, you're better than that. What I mean is, he doesn't like slow bowling.'

'Hang on a minute, I'm not that slow.'

By now the rest of the lads were pissing themselves laughing. But Goughie insisted on making his point: 'You're slower than the rest of us and he likes to have the ball come on to him so he can use the pace. I'm telling you, he won't like facing you, especially if the keeper's up.'

It turned out he was dead right. I had a really good series against Sachin, especially in the first Lord's match. I was trying to get in his face and break his concentration. It wasn't my style to swear or have a go at batsmen. I liked to look them in the eye and maybe have a joke with them, let them know I was confident and enjoying taking them on. He wasn't having any of it, so the next time he was at the bowler's end I said, 'Hey, Sachin, you've always struggled against my bowling. Why's that? You're number one in the world and you're not hitting me off the square. How come?'

To my surprise, he bit and hit me with the best comeback I ever received. 'Ronnie,' he said, 'this is my 305th one-day international. Believe me, I like your bowling.'

I thought, Oh fuck, what have I done? I feared I'd poked a stick in a hornets' nest and my confidence wasn't helped when I said to Graham Thorpe at mid-on, 'Did you hear that?'

'Yeah. Tell Nasser to get you off quick. In fact, don't finish the over. Go off sick.'

'Fuck off, I've broken him. No one's managed to get a word out of him and now I've destroyed his concentration.'

'No, dickhead. You've just persuaded the world number-one batsman that he has to prove how much he enjoys your bowling. How many more balls, umpire?'

'Shut up, I've got him.' I didn't actually believe it but as it turned out it was true.

They nicked a single off my next ball and then I ran in to bowl to Sachin. The ball took the slope, nipped back and cracked against his knee roll. The whole team went up in a massive appeal. Even Freddie Flintoff at square leg knew it was plumb. I didn't give a toss about technicalities: if you can get past Sachin Tendulkar's bat and hit him on the pad, that's out for me. And Neil Mallender – what a great umpire – agreed and stuck his finger in the air.

The only person with no inkling that it could be out was Sachin, who was trying to sneak a single. As he raced down the pitch, he met me coming the other way with my back to him, still triumphantly yelling my appeal. And that is how a jockey-sized batsman knocked a 6ft 4in bowler on his arse in the middle of the pitch. As I got up and dusted myself off, I called out, 'Hey, Sachin, this is my fifth one-day international and I like your batting!' I don't think he heard me above the tumult from the crowd. When India play at Lord's the whole Indian community in London seems to turn out, so it was no real surprise that, when the England hero made his way to the boundary after the over, he was booed for dismissing the little master.

Despite my triumph and a great knock from Marcus Trescothick, we lost the match with seven balls to go.

We scored a second win over Sri Lanka at Headingley and I was really beginning to feel at home as an England player again. I was promoted to bat at three to hurry things along and managed to hit a useful 27 in as many balls. Our next match against India at the Riverside was eventually washed out but not before Tendulkar had smashed an unbeaten century. However, as I pointed out to Darren Gough, he never hit one boundary off my bowling.

A surprise defeat by Sri Lanka at Old Trafford meant we needed to beat India at the Oval and it turned out to be one of the greatest days of my life. Again I was promoted to bat at three and it worked like a dream. I saw the ball as big as a football and was able to steer it all round the ground. I reached my first international half-century in 55 balls, helping to take England from 52-1 to 202-5, but in the end we were only defending 229 against one of the most prolific batting line-ups in the world.

At the start of the series, I'd asked Stewie to stand up to the stumps when I bowled. He'd been unsure because some bowlers feel it demeans them to have the keeper up. I didn't care about that. Thanks to Andy Flower, I'd seen how it helped my chances and I was more concerned about taking wickets than whether some people thought I was too slow. India were looking good at 62-1 with Virender Sehwag scoring at faster than a run a ball, but I managed to find the edge of his bat and Alec took a sharp chance. He then stumped Yuvraj Singh off my bowling and in one mind-blowing five-ball spell I took three more wickets – one of them caught by Alec – without conceding a run. My team-mates mobbed me and I couldn't remember feeling more fulfilled on a cricket pitch. The crowd absolutely loved it and went mad every time I went back to the boundary. I felt on an incredible high and so proud when I saw the delight on my dad's face as he sat among the fans who were singing my name. It was less than a year since his major operation and the fact that he was there to share in my great day meant everything to me.

The icing on the cake came when their number-eleven batsman Ashish Nehra hoisted Alex Tudor towards long on and I managed to make up the ground and take the final catch of the match. With Alec Stewart excelling behind the stumps, we had bowled them out and I became only the second Englishman (with Graeme Hick) to take five wickets and score 50 runs in the same match. My bowling figures of 5-26 are still a world record for an ODI at the Oval.

The next day the back pages of the papers carried huge pictures of me, banner headlines and reports all agreeing that I had left the international wilderness and was now back in the mainstream. Suddenly people who had written me off as 'enthusiastic but not quite good enough' were saying I might be one of the keys to our World Cup chances. Most satisfying was when I watched the highlights on TV and heard David Lloyd, the man who had turned against me on tour, say, 'Ronnie Irani has even taken the last catch. You can't keep the lad out of the game.'

The win set up what turned out to be a thrilling final at Lord's between us and India when they got their revenge in a feast of runs. Marcus Trescothick and Nasser Hussain scored centuries as we piled on 325 in our 50 overs. That should have been ample to win the match but Nass had made the mistake of sledging Mohammad Kaif in an earlier match, asking him if he was Sachin's kit man, and the Indian batsman took his revenge. I was one of the bowlers he smashed all round the ground as he hit 87 in 75 balls. Even though we had knocked over Tendulkar and Dravid cheaply, Yuvraj Singh and Kaif battered us and India got home with three balls to spare. It was disappointing not to win the tournament but a very important few weeks for me were crowned when I was voted the Fans Player of the Tournament. I liked to think they knew I would always fight to the final ball for my country and was chuffed the Barmy Army had taken to me as one of their own, just as the Essex crowd had.

The selectors obviously saw me as a one-day player because they didn't pick me for the Test series that summer, but I was quite happy to go back to Essex and help them win promotion for the second time in three years, confident that

I had done enough to earn a place in the World Cup squad that winter. What I didn't realise was that politics were going to play as big a part as cricket.

CHAPTER 20

A LONG STRETCH
IN SYDNEY

It was going to be a busy winter for England cricketers. There was the small matter of an Ashes and ODI series Down Under before moving on to South Africa for the 2003 World Cup. I'd come to terms with the fact that I was no longer considered a five-day player by the selectors so I wasn't at all surprised when the radio announced that I was to be part of the squad for an ICC one-day tournament in Sri Lanka intended as preparation for the World Cup. You can therefore imagine my shock when a letter landed on the mat that said: 'Congratulations, you've been chosen to tour Australia with England.' It went on to tell me where and when to report and what my fee would be. According to this, I was in the Test party. I immediately suspected a cock-up and, even though Lorraine pointed out it was a contract and I should just turn up at the airport and see what they said, I decided to phone David Graveney.

He was very embarrassed and said, 'Err, sorry, Ronnie, that's a mistake. That wasn't meant to go to you. Just tear it up. I'm really sorry.'

With the World Cup coming up I wasn't in the mood to rock the boat, so I threw the letter in the bin, but to this day I've never resolved if it was just incompetence or if I had originally been selected and someone had put the block on.

The Sri Lanka trip was hard work. The heat was so oppressive it burned your throat. Dominic Cork and I knew we were on trial for a place in Australia and the World Cup so, even though it felt as though there wasn't enough air to fill your lungs when you bowled, we had to keep galloping in. If anything, I think Dom tried too hard and he missed out when it was announced who would join up with the squad for the ODIs in Australia. Personally I would have taken him because he was still a good enough bowler to change games.

We got a drubbing in Sri Lanka. I scored a few runs against India and managed to pick up four wickets against Zimbabwe, including Andy Flower. His brother Grant restored family honour by getting me out sweeping. But, as I'd hoped, my name was down for Australia along with Nick Knight, James Kirtley and Jeremy Snape.

The news from the Ashes tour was all bad. England were being taken apart and the media were starting to be very negative back home. I did some interviews before I left and, when I was asked if I was dreading what I would find, I replied, 'Actually I'm looking forward to the series. It's a golden opportunity for me. Everybody's saying, "Oh, God, you're going to get your arses whipped, sheep to the slaughter." Well, bollocks, wolves in sheep's clothing, that's what you've got to hope. We can't be all doom and gloom, thinking, Yeah here comes a pounding. No way. I don't train hard, leave my family behind, live every minute of the day for the game, to come here hoping, if it all goes well, I'll be back in one piece. I'm thinking, I'm up for it – let's get it on.'

It all sounded great as I said it and I meant every word. But I admit to a moment's concern when I saw the banner headline in the *Sun* which read: 'B****CKS TO AUSSIES: Ronnie rallies England with one-day battle cry' and wondered if I might have just stirred up the chaps in the baggy green caps even more than usual. But then I thought, Sod it. That's how they play cricket. Let's show them we can be in your face too.

The England camp was certainly at a low ebb when we joined up with them. Only Freddie Flintoff, who was getting himself fit again after injury, was his usual lively self. The energy he puts into cricket is also applied to his social life. I recall him picking up four beer bottles between his fingers, somehow getting all the necks to his mouth at once and downing the contents. I've also seen him drink a bottle of champagne in one go and give out the biggest belch I've ever heard. In Adelaide, he asked me for ten dollars and, when I asked him what it was for, he said, 'Champagne.' When I pointed out that you couldn't buy bubbly for ten bucks, he replied, 'No, but it will get me into the Crazy Horse and I'll put the rest on my card.' But Freddie's an outstanding cricketer. He is a quick and accurate bowler and a clean hitter of the ball. I always enjoyed taking him on when we played against each other. The only downside was that, while he liked to give out stick, he wasn't great at taking it.

I have to say I love the way Australians play cricket. They are tough, they are ruthless and they are desperate to win. They will try to intimidate you but afterwards they will buy you a beer. They also have a lot of time for people who will stand up to them and give them a game. I witnessed one of the best examples of how cricket should be played in the warm-up game against New South Wales at the Sydney

Cricket Ground. Stuart McGill, a magnificent spinner who would have won many more caps if he hadn't been unfortunate enough to be the same generation as Shane Warne, was bowling to me and I played a terrific shot to the boundary. He just quietly said, 'Good shot.' The next ball was such a beauty I wasn't good enough to even get an edge. That's great cricket.

The other side of the Aussies, of course, is that they are mouthy bastards who never know when to shut up. I realised they too had seen the headline in the *Sun* when I faced a barrage of abuse as I walked out to bat. They knew I was under pressure and fighting for my World Cup place, and Glenn McGrath greeted me with 'You're going to get a duck, Irani.'

I was again batting three and expected to move things along but I didn't want to risk throwing away my wicket so it took me some time to get off the mark. After each ball, I'd hear McGrath chuntering, 'You're going to get a duck, Irani. No problem. Big fat duck.'

I managed to knock one into the offside and was looking for a quick single to get me going but Steve Waugh swooped on the ball and yelled, 'Fucking get back, pommie!' and proceeded to give me a gobful of abuse.

I was beginning to think McGrath might be right but then I told myself that, if they were going to this length to put me off, they must rate me. So I gritted my teeth and smiled so they couldn't tell if they were getting to me. Brett Lee came steaming in. He was rapid and, with the keeper rabbiting in my ear behind me, it wasn't easy to concentrate. The ball reared up towards my head and I pivoted to hook it. Instead, I got a top edge that flew over the slip fielders' heads and crashed against the boundary board. 'I say, old boy, that was rather fortunate,' was not quite how the Aussies put it, but it was the gist of what they meant. I went on to make 80 very satisfying runs.

Bowling in the NSW innings wasn't as much fun as batting had been. Nasser was determined we were going to use the game to practise how we would play in the World Cup and everyone, including the Aussie batsmen, could hear him yell, 'You've got to practise yorkers.'

Now, Steve Waugh is one of the finest batsmen his country has produced. Bowling to him in front of his home crowd in Sydney, where he is considered a god, is hard enough without telling him exactly where the ball is going to pitch. It's uncanny in Sydney: the crowd seem to almost whisper his name, but with 12,000 people that makes for a very weird, almost mystic sound. That became a roar when he took his left leg out of the way and despatched my next yorker for the biggest six I've ever seen. Thanks, Nass. The home fans had a wonderful afternoon's entertainment as Steve battered us around and won them the game, the final runs an unstoppable boundary off my bowling.

There are some great stadiums where cricket is played, like the MCG in Melbourne, but for me Sydney is the ultimate cricket ground. It has character and a wonderful, old-fashioned pavilion. It is helped by being in a fantastic city where you always need mirror sunglasses on the beach so no one, especially your wife, can see where you are looking. Steve Waugh is one of the city's greatest sons, along with his younger brother – by four minutes – Mark. Both have that irresistible combination of talent and will to win that I like in a player. They back themselves to do well every time they cross the boundary rope and you just know they would have succeeded at whatever sport or occupation they had taken up in life. Frank Dick always used to say that, when faced with a team full of really good players, a coach didn't necessarily look to see who was the most talented but which of them was most willing to fine-tune and improve their skills. That was the Waugh brothers.

I only had a few chances to talk to Steve but was always impressed by his knowledge and thought he was a great bloke to share a beer with. I got to know Mark really well because he was Essex's overseas player soon after I joined. We only played together for a year but I could happily have played cricket with him every single day of my life. What an attitude! I remember turning up at Colchester for a match when he was struggling with a groin strain. 'I'm playing, mate,' he said. 'There's 140 just for the taking in that wicket.' He scored a century. He didn't care who the opposition were: he was confident he would come out on top and usually did.

Mark always had a smile on his face and a kind spirit. As a teenager, I'd played with another of the brothers, Dean Waugh, who tore bowlers apart in the Bolton League and had a fair career but was always in the shadow of the twins. Mark was always generous when talking about Dean and I sensed he would have loved it if all three brothers could have played in the same Aussie side. Mark enjoyed a good time, loved a bet and particularly loved his cricket. I always relished his company and one of my ambitions is to go back to Australia with the family and spend some time with him, maybe even challenge him to a game of golf for a few dollars. He wouldn't be able to resist that.

The ODIs were a disappointment. I had a bad series but that was partly because my mind wasn't completely on my cricket. It had been arranged that wives and families would fly out shortly before Christmas but I got a call from Lorraine telling me she had suffered a third miscarriage. I have never felt so far away from home in my life. I longed to be with her because I knew how much she would be hurting. She put on a brave face and told me not to worry. 'Concentrate on your cricket. The girls and I will come out as soon as we can.' But I could tell she was really longing for a hug. I was concerned how the girls were coping – they were too young to understand what had happened but they would certainly sense something was wrong and this was just the time when Lorraine would need Daddy to take them out while she came to terms with her own grief.

It was harder to deal with because none of my close mates was there to help – no Tuffers, Thorpe or Gough. I felt lonely and I felt guilty. For several nights I cried myself to sleep, knowing that, as much as I loved playing cricket, it isn't the be all and end all in life. But, after everything that had happened on other tours, I didn't want to show any weakness to the management so I kept things bottled up. Strangely, the people I was best able to talk to during this time were some of my Aussie friends.

Not everyone approved of my willingness to be matey with the opposition once we were off the pitch. Just as in the Tests, the Aussies were taking us to the cleaners in the ODIs and enjoying every minute of it. After a reasonable first match, I was struggling to score runs and in Sydney was dismissed for a duck. I knew several of the Aussie team – I'd met Ricky Ponting and Brett Lee through Mark Waugh, played against Adam Gilchrist in the U19s, and against Matthew Hayden when he was in the Bolton League with Greenmount and later with Hampshire and Northants. After the match, I shook hands with Ricky and he said, 'If you fancy a drink, mate, come in our changing room. No problem.'

Our dressing room was as flat as stale beer. The only voice was Nasser's telling us how shit we all were. When he'd finished I put on my trainers and went to leave the room. Alec Stewart asked where I was going and when I said, 'Next door for a beer,' he decided to join me, as did young Owais Shah. Some would see it as consorting with the enemy but I've always felt, if you get to know an opponent as an ordinary bloke with whom you get on socially, you don't fear him as much when you are head to head out on the pitch.

It also gives you a chance to talk cricket to some of the best players in the world and you can learn from that. I'm sure that, once he was able to get over his awe at having a beer with Shane Warne, Owais learned a lot that day. Before long, most of the England team had followed us into the Aussie dressing room and it was a good craic. The thing that surprised me was that the lads said this was the first time they had socialised with the Aussies during the tour.

We'd been in there about an hour when Nick Knight, who had popped out for a minute, came back and announced, 'You're not going to believe this but Nass and Duncan Fletcher have fucked off on the team bus and left us here.'

I think it is fair to say the lads were not chuffed. They knew Nass would not want to go in the Aussie dressing room but thought he might have just given us a heads-up that they were leaving. As it was, they had just provided the Aussies with something else to sledge us about. We got our gear together and made our way back to the hotel in cabs. When we arrived, Nass was sitting at the bar. I called across, 'Thanks for waiting for us, Nass.'

'Serves you right, sucking up to the Aussies. Big mates, are we?'

'Yeah, as it happens. I like some of them better than some of the people I've played with.'

'Well, you go ahead and kiss their arse. But don't expect the rest of us to hang about while you do it. While I'm in charge of the team, you get on the bus and go back to the hotel and, if you don't like it, you know what you can do.'

I just shrugged and said, 'No worries, pal.' I really couldn't understand his reasoning. To me, his attitude was a sign of weakness, having to build artificial antagonism against your opponent. Partly, I think, it was because he was a bit of a loner and preferred his own company. Quite often if you rang him in the hotel and asked if he wanted to go to dinner, he'd say, 'What's it to you?' and eat alone. He really would have been happier as a tennis player. For me, the contest out in the middle was more than enough to fire me up. On the pitch I will fight for the badge as hard as anyone, perhaps harder than some. I hate to lose – it's why I believe I've always enjoyed a rapport with the fans – but I don't hate the guys I'm playing against. I can see nothing wrong in mixing with the opposition when the battle's over. After all, the Aussies do it and it doesn't seem to undermine their performances.

Lorraine, her mum and the girls finally arrived on Christmas Day. I went to the airport at eight o'clock in the morning to meet them. I was feeling very emotional, partly because of the miscarriage and the fact that I had expected to have three children by then, but also at missing out on the kids waking up on Christmas morning and unwrapping their parcels. Bizarrely, my wait was cheered up by a group of the Barmy Army, slightly the worse for wear, who wanted to chat and have photos taken. I don't know why they were there and none of them asked me what the hell I was doing sitting round an airport lounge on Christmas Day. They probably thought I was a secret plane spotter. It was so great to see the family but of course they were completely knackered after the flight and they slept the whole of Christmas. But it was a relief to be together again at last and we enjoyed some fantastic times over the next few weeks. We must have been to every beach in Adelaide, Melbourne and Sydney and it was just so satisfying to be a family once more.

As well as the Aussie players, I was getting on well with the local fans, or most of them. It was during the Sydney ODI that the famous stretching incident took place, which now has more than 35,000 viewings on YouTube, far more than any shot I've made or ball I've bowled! We were getting hammered and Nasser had shouted down to me to take the next over at the far end, so I started to warm up. I'd already had a bit of banter with the crowd and, as I started to stretch, I became aware of a lot of laughter behind me. I thought it was one of their usual pranks like punching a beach ball around and shouting out each time it soars into the air, or their other favourite, putting hundreds of plastic pint glasses inside each other and then hoisting them aloft like a giant snake. I glanced behind me and realised that the whole section were on their feet and copying my warm-up. They were loving it so I played to the gallery for a bit and even Nasser and the rest of the lads were laughing.

What is missing from the video and is usually forgotten is that, a couple of minutes later, a rather well-endowed young lady came out of the crowd wearing nothing but a smile and asked me to autograph her breasts. Like most sports people, I've managed to perfect a signature that I can repeat very quickly as I make my way through a crowd outside the dressing room. However, I didn't want to damage this particular autograph book so I took my time, making sure I dotted all the 'i's. And the grin on my usual smiley face was so large it was almost a leer!

It was amazing how quickly the stretching incident caught the imagination. A few days later, when I was on the beach with the family, three hefty lads came towards us. I was a bit nervous in case they were looking for bother. Instead, they took photos out of their wallets and pointed themselves out among the crowd stretching behind me and asked me to sign them. Of course I obliged, although now my signature was back to its usual speed. A few days later, I was in Canberra captaining an England XI against a Don Bradman XI led by Mark Waugh. He and I had a night out and were in a taxi waiting to go to a restaurant when a guy banged on the window and said, 'Irani, you're a legend. You're a champion, dude!' I was a bit embarrassed because I happened to be sitting next to a real Aussie legend and it was a while before the guy recognised him and said, 'Shit, Waughy! You're a champion too!'

Of course, you can't please all the people all the time and there were a few Australians who didn't think I was the coolest thing since Fosters straight from the fridge. It especially didn't go down well when I dismissed Shane Warne in his last ODI on his home ground in Melbourne. It was a sweltering hot day and Nasser had insisted on bowling me for ten straight overs. I was knackered. Shane came in and received a standing ovation all the way to the wicket. They loved him. That got my adrenaline pumping again and I steamed in and got one to zip back. Normally, Shane would have fended it off but he wanted to please his fans and went for a big drive. Instead, he got an inside edge that came back to me and I caught it. I threw the ball in the air in triumph and realised there was total silence around the ground. It only lasted a few seconds before the Victoria crowd went berserk and, as Paul Simon said, I heard words I never heard in the Bible.

I went back to fielding in front of the MCG members. A guy who had been gradually getting more and more drunk as the day went on had already been giving me some abuse but now he was really wound up. 'Irani, you're a shit cricketer. Look at you, you're a tosser.' It went on and on, ball after ball.

At first I thought the stewards were bound to intervene but they did nothing and, as much as I tried to ignore him, it was starting to annoy me. Finally, I'd had enough and decided to have a word. I felt like thumping him to be honest but I knew I had to be careful and not let it go too far. I also knew that anyone who goes on the pitch at the MCG automatically gets a $5,000 fine and reckoned I might be able to hit him in the pocket if not the mouth. I picked up my drink bottle and headed towards the stand. He'd gone quiet suddenly and I wasn't really sure which of the sea of faces was his. I picked one guy out and said, 'I'm sick and tired of you abusing me.'

He looked perplexed and a doubt crept into my mind. I was about to turn on my heel and walk away when I heard the familiar dulcet tones: 'Irani, you're a wanker.'

He'd come right to the fence to abuse me again and, as he launched into his tirade, I said, 'You need to cool off, pal.'

'Oh yeah? What you gonna do about it?'

I took the water bottle and threw the lot over him. He was soaked.

'Come on,' I said. 'You're a big guy. Come here and have your say.'

Any minute now, his abuse would cost him five grand but just as he was about to climb over the fence the stewards finally intervened and dragged him away.

Crowds in England have a drink but they seldom get abusive. Up in Yorkshire they like to give you a verbal volley but it's all banter and, if you give them a smile, they are fine. Even though the MCG lot are usually hostile – I've had a golf ball and a barbecue chicken thrown at me – most of them are OK underneath it all. At one stage they started a chant: 'Ronnie Irani' clap, clap, clap, 'you are a wanker' clap, clap, clap. I gave them a wave and did a forward roll. They loved it and started cheering me.

At least these moments took my mind off the hammering we were getting and the effect that would have on my chances of making the World Cup squad. When it was finally announced, I was both delighted and relieved to see my name in the 15. There were a few surprise omissions. As I've said, Dominic Cork would have been a useful guy to have along, as would Robert Key. Rob was on the Australian trip but somehow his face didn't fit. I thought he was not just a fine bowler, but also a very clever cricketer and a canny captain. He steered Kent to twenty20 success as much on his nous as anything else and he was the only player in my time leading Essex who beat me in a match just by his captaincy. It was a one-day game at Chelmsford and Rob completely outwitted me with his tactics. If it had been my decision, he would have been the England captain when Michael Vaughan stepped down.

But the cut-off point had to fall somewhere and Rob was just on the other side of it. But before I tell you about South Africa, this might be a good place for Lorraine to explain something of what it is like to be a cricketer's wife.

CHAPTER 21
AT TIMES IT'S LIKE BEING A SINGLE MUM
BY LORRAINE

Ronnie and I have been together since we were little more than kids. In many ways we have grown up together and we've been fortunate because we haven't moved in opposite directions. Not that it's been all chocolates and roses – there have been plenty of times when I've been ready to pack his bag or mine – but, on the whole, we have been very lucky. I still occasionally look at the wonderful house we have, our two special daughters and the lifestyle we are able to enjoy and wonder how it all happened to kids from Bolton who started off with just a few bob they had scraped together.

We were still teenagers when we uprooted to Essex. It was scary but I'd been brought up to believe that you should follow your dream, and the only way Ronnie could do that was to switch counties and he chose Essex. I moved first and went to Buckinghamshire. He'd encouraged me to study in my spare time and become a qualified nursery nurse and I got a job in Aylesbury to be near him. Well, they looked close on the map!

I'm quite glad I did it that way because it meant I had a short time living on my own, so I've never had that nagging feeling at the back of my mind, wondering what it would have been like to be completely independent. It wasn't really my cup of tea. I'm a bit of an old-fashioned, home-loving girl and I was happy to move into a flat with him at first in Colchester and then Writtle. The move south was made much easier by the fact that Essex is a friendly, family club. I'd never really felt at home at Old Trafford when Ronnie was with Lancashire but they made us very welcome at Chelmsford and some of the people there have become close friends and watched us and our family grow up together.

After a couple of years renting, we decided to buy our first place – a dream cottage in Great Waltham that cost us £132,500. I couldn't get my head round that kind of money – back in Bolton you could buy a whole street for that, and I still find the north-south price differences startling. We stretched ourselves to the max for a mortgage and could only afford the bare basics in furniture. I know both families were anxious about the size of the mortgage we were hanging round our necks.

The financial burden was helped by Ronnie being selected for his first England tour. It was a relief to get the extra money but was something of a turning point in my life. He'd been away before, of course, but I'd always been at home with my mum. This was different. I was alone in a strange house, with no alarm system and no friends or family anywhere near. I remember thinking that I could die and it would be a long time before anyone found me. I didn't want to worry Mum and I'd learned already that, when your husband is working away, it's not a good time to burden him with your problems, especially when you know that things are not working out so well for him and he is anxious about his career. You just put on a brave front and do your crying alone when you go to bed. Luckily I found I had two wonderful neighbours, Jack and Kit, who took me under their wing and became like my granny and grandpa. But there were still many, many lonely and scary hours in the house on my own.

I had two choices: get used to it or get out, and I didn't want to get out. But it meant I needed to become good at things I'd never had to think about before, be self-sufficient and independent. And that meant that, by the time Ronnie came back from tour, I had changed. As you can imagine, the first few days you are back together fly by in wonderful fashion, almost like a new love affair. But then Ronnie started to notice little things that had changed in me. I was used to making the decisions and getting things done and I still wanted to do that. As I didn't always do things the way he would, I began to understand why cricket has one of the highest divorce rates of any sport.

Eventually, we had to sit down and thrash it out. I said, 'You can't expect me to change back to the person I was just because you have come home. I've sat here at nights and cried because I was scared. I came to terms with that and learned to cope. I had to become a different person, stronger and more self-reliant. I need to be like that because you will be going away again.' To my relief, Ronnie accepted it.

As Ronnie has told you, it took him ten years to get round to proposing but I really didn't mind because I didn't feel either of us needed a ring to feel committed to each other. I became pregnant shortly after we got married and we were both very excited because we wanted children. We were due to go to South Africa but then I miscarried. It was traumatic.

I didn't really know what was happening and again didn't want to phone Mum and worry her. It is hard to describe the sense of loss you have when you lose a baby, a life that you have become aware is growing inside you. I felt grief, anger and guilt, sometimes all at the same time. It put a doubt in my mind that we would ever be able to have children and I wondered how that would change our hopes and our relationship. It changed my whole perspective on life.

The second time it happened was in the middle of the cricket season, just after Ronnie took over as captain of Essex. I knew he was having problems with some of the members of the squad and needed to be at the ground sorting things out. I almost had to force him out the door, telling him there was nothing he could do at home, but it was always good when he came back and we could just hold each other. By this time, I'd become quite good at keeping things back so as not to distract Ronnie, to wait until the end of a match before raising something that needed sorting out. He's a very positive, larger-than-life man most of the time and great fun to be around, but, if he's got a problem, he can't leave it alone and I could always tell from his face when the game was not going as well as it might. In fact, he was harder on himself than that – he expected so much of himself that he could be dissatisfied even when others thought he'd had a great day.

I suffered from panic attacks after losing the second baby and that's when we got Eric the Doberman. He was my rock, a gem who was great company when Ronnie was away. Shortly after that I fell pregnant with Simone. As Ronnie has told you, we had bought the old house in Felsted and it wasn't nearly as comfortable as the one we'd left, but we were willing to put up with that because we had a dream of what could be. Ronnie was in Germany getting treatment when I discovered I was pregnant and my first instinct was to phone him and tell him. But I knew he'd fly home and I told myself, 'In the past, you've done everything by the book, put your feet up and taken care, and you've lost both babies. Just behave normally and let whatever is going to happen happen.' So I just got on with packing the house away and told him when he returned home at the weekend. We were both nervous but didn't say so. Fortunately it all went smoothly and Simone was born, quickly followed by Maria. Life had changed again, but in a very positive way.

We had hoped to have a big family but that was obviously not going to be when I had a third miscarriage. It was the worst of the lot because Ronnie was on the other side of the world. With the World Cup coming up, I didn't want him to fly home, although I was longing to be with him. I was lucky to have the support of my mum and eventually we all flew out together on Christmas Day. It was the strangest Christmas I've ever known. The girls were only two and one and, with Ronnie having been away for some time, they weren't really sure who he was and just wanted to cling to their mum and granny. I'm sure it hurt Ronnie at first but he soon won them round and we had a really wonderful holiday.

As the girls grew up, we again had to make adjustments in our marriage. At times it was like being a single parent. Even in England, cricketers work long hours during the season and, when he became captain, Ronnie would often not get home until after the girls had gone to bed. He missed much of their childhood and so would want to spoil them whenever he was with them. Finally, I had to point out that I couldn't always be the 'bad cop' who disciplined them and said no, while he was the 'good cop' who always brought them presents and agreed to what they wanted. And everything would go awry if I'd made a decision while he was away and they were able to change it on appeal when he returned. We gradually sorted out the rules. We've been very lucky and have two girls we are both incredibly proud of.

I guess being married to a cricketer is not the kind of life that I had planned when my school friends and I used to discuss our dreams for the future. It's silly things that you notice, like being the only one not in a couple when friends invite you to a barbecue in the summer and Ronnie is away playing in Durham or Glamorgan. It was also strange not being able to take summer holidays together when the children were off school. The nearest we got was when Essex played at South Church Park in Southend. We would stay in a bed and breakfast nearby, park the car and forget about it for the week. We'd walk to and from the ground, pop to the Adventure Island or take the girls out on their bikes. After play, we'd have fish and chips in the café in the park. It will probably seem strange to some people when I say that we've been to some wonderful places with Ronnie, like Australia, but those days in Southend were among the most enjoyable just because they were so normal.

I've always tried to stay in the background of Ronnie's career and think some of the WAGS give the rest of us a bad name. I've never understood why they think there should be any attention on them. If their husband was a greengrocer, they wouldn't hang around the shop looking for the limelight, so why do it when your husband plays cricket or football?

As I've said, we were very lucky that Essex is such a friendly place. Simone and Maria wanted to see as much of their dad as possible so we spent a lot of time at Chelmsford when he had a home match. There was a room set aside where we could go with the kids so we became friendly with the other players' families – though some of the younger guys changed girlfriends so often I found it hard to remember all the names! But, as well as the players and the staff, we got to know a lot of the supporters and they would play with the girls and give them sweets. It became an extended family.

I didn't realise how much I would miss it all when Ronnie was forced to quit. It was so abrupt. I got depressed and kept bursting into tears for a while. Essex County Cricket Club had become such a big part of our lives and suddenly it was no longer there. The girls found it hard to understand at first. It was also a slightly worrying time because Ronnie had to carve out a whole new career at an age when most people are well established. The job at talkSPORT has been tremendous for him and works out wonderfully for the family because we see a lot more of him, though he's often a bit yawny by the early evening.

As I say, it's not the kind of marriage I had envisaged but I wouldn't change it. It's made me a stronger person and I've enjoyed being the hub of our family, the one who is always there. I'm fortunate in that I work in the family business Ronnie and I are developing and that allows me to be at home when the girls are there. I'm lucky to have Mum living with us and helping me, which gives me the opportunity to pursue interests like running our local Brownie pack. And it's very satisfying watching the girls growing into very nice people, with all their dad's determination to succeed but also his love of life.

Being a cricketer's wife is not something I would recommend to everyone and a lot of women have found it impossible. I've been one of the fortunate ones for whom it has worked out all right.

CHAPTER 22
THE GAME THAT NEVER WAS

On arriving in South Africa, the England party were given a few days off in Sun City to put their feet up and play some golf before getting back down to business in the World Cup. The theory was that we'd already had a long, difficult trip and needed a break from cricket. It seemed a weird decision to me. We were just going into arguably the biggest matches of our lives and, even if they wanted us to rest physically, this seemed like the perfect time to talk tactics, watch videos and work out how we were going to play the opposition.

One of the shortcomings of England cricket is that we don't handle defeat well. Instead of analysing things and trying to fathom out how to get better, the instinct seems to be to drop one or two players, hunker down and hope it gets better next time. My own view is that, if you have your best players together, you keep working on them until they come good. I remember all the calls before football's Euro 96 for Alan Shearer to be dropped because he was having a lean spell in front of goal. Terry Venables stuck with him,

Shearer found his form and almost took the side to the final. It's a cliché but it's also true that form is temporary but class is permanent.

I decided R&R wasn't for me. I hadn't been away as long as the rest of them and I wanted to work on my game. I'd had a poor series in Australia and I wanted to get back in top nick before what would hopefully be a memorable World Cup and I didn't think that playing golf would help. Some of my team-mates didn't seem too pleased when I said I was going to stay in Port Elizabeth. Perhaps they thought I was trying to earn brownie points with Duncan Fletcher and the coaches but they needn't have worried: I was also getting negative vibes from the management because it meant they had to make special arrangements. However, it was hard for them to argue against someone wanting to get into peak condition. I just thought, Bollocks to the lot of them. This is probably my only chance to play in a World Cup and I want to be ready. I can play as much golf as I want after my cricket is over.

None of the coaching staff volunteered to stay with me, so I turned to Ian Pont at Essex. He had been a bowler himself and had a brief spell as baseball pitcher in the States. Since retiring from playing, he'd been involved in the production of the first coloured cricket kits and had become a dynamic coach with new ideas. He'd already had a big effect on my bowling by applying his understanding of biomechanics. I'd watched him coaching some of the young guys at Essex – particularly Maurice Chambers and Mervyn Westfield, who could both play for England one day – and realised that, if I'd worked with Ian at their age, my bowling would have gone to a whole new level and I might not have had so many problems with injuries. I rang him, explained the situation and said, 'Is there any chance you could come out here for a week? I'll pay all your bills.' Despite all the things he had on his plate, he didn't hesitate. He cancelled his plans and flew straight out.

Typically of South Africans, the ground staff at Port Elizabeth couldn't have been more helpful. Nothing was too much trouble for them. The authorities also supplied us with an armed guard who came everywhere with us, a loaded revolver on his hip. He became part of the team for the week. Fortunately he never had to use his gun.

Ian and I got through a lot of work on both batting and bowling. By the time the rest of the squad came back from Sun City, I was feeling happier about my game and up for the challenge. We had a couple of warm-up matches and I took a few wickets but you didn't need to be Russell Grant to work out that Craig White was going to be first-choice all-rounder, despite the fact that he was recovering from an injury. But there was something even bigger that looked like standing in the way of my childhood dream of representing England in the World Cup. Politics.

We flew down to Cape Town for the opening ceremony, which was staged at Newlands in some style, but it was overshadowed for the England lads by the row that had been brewing for some time about whether or not we should play the match scheduled for Zimbabwe. This was at the time when it was becoming generally accepted that Robert Mugabe's regime was one of the most oppressive in the world and there were plenty of people ready to advise us what we should do. Several pressure groups in England felt it would be immoral for us to play there, claiming it would seem that we were endorsing an evil despot. The British government also made it clear they didn't want us to go but being mealy-mouthed politicians they insisted it wasn't their place to stop us. The ECB didn't want to pull out because they might face a hefty fine, rumoured to be $10million. The ICC, who were organising the tournament, could see nothing but the problems they would have with TV companies and sponsors if the games had to be moved, and were threatening that we would lose the points if we failed to go.

So, while everyone seemed to have a strong opinion, if anyone was going to take a stand on moral grounds, it was down to us. Cricketers would have to put principles above their desire to play in the World Cup. The turkeys would have to vote for Christmas.

I've never been political and have to admit that I always read a newspaper from the back. I don't take much interest in domestic politics let alone international affairs, but I knew something of the situation in Zimbabwe from conversations I'd had in Australia with BBC correspondent Pat Murphy. He is big on human rights and felt passionately that we should not support Mugabe's regime by playing in Zimbabwe. He'd already told the BBC he wouldn't cover the match if it were played. He explained to me about some of the atrocities that went on there, the beatings, torture, rape and murder, and my first thought was why the hell has nothing been done about this before? Why is it being left to cricketers to bring pressure on Mugabe? What had the world leaders being doing about it?

We were staying in the Cullinan Hotel, an impressive building near Cape Town's waterfront and within sight of Table Mountain. It had everything you could want from a hotel but it was hard to enjoy our stay because we were constantly under the cloud of the Zimbabwe controversy. It was the only topic of conversation among the players, even though the other matches were now only days away, and the situation became even more pressurised when the ECB announced they had received a message from a group calling themselves the Sons and Daughters of Zimbabwe. The letter said that, however much we might condemn the regime, if we travelled to Harare we would still be 'wittingly or unwittingly taking part in Mugabe's propaganda'. It went on: 'Our message to you is simple: COME TO ZIMBABWE AND YOU WILL GO BACK TO BRITAIN IN WOODEN COFFINS.' The letter finished: 'Our advice is this: DON'T COME TO ZIMBABWE OR YOUR PLAYERS WILL BE LIVING IN FEAR FOR THE REST OF THEIR LIVES.'

That concentrated a lot of minds and was enough for several players to decide they definitely didn't want to go. We had meeting after meeting. The World Cup security people assured us there was no danger – 'We'll have a jet waiting and, if we have to get you out, we'll get you out.' Then we were summoned to a meeting with the Australian chief executive of the ICC, Malcolm Speed, who didn't seem to give a toss about what we thought and told us that, if we didn't play, Zimbabwe would be awarded the match. Nasser had many fine points as a captain and he has a great record, but calm negotiation is not one of his strong suits. He ended up having a slanging match with Speed and completely lost it. He yelled, 'I want to know where my wife and children are right now and if they're safe! That's what I care about at this moment, not your fucking World Cup!'

There was an extraordinary atmosphere: players were in tears, and some people you'd think would be the first to defy the odds were among the most timid.

I was totally confused and went off to my room to think out my own position. I took it as read that nothing we did should show support for Mugabe and his henchmen. But I was very doubtful that 11 Englishmen failing to turn up for a cricket match would make an ounce of difference to a man who was willing to condone the murder of his fellow citizens. People said that the sporting boycott of South Africa helped bring apartheid to an end but it seemed to me the collapse of that oppression had been much more to do with a guy called Nelson Mandela. And I couldn't help thinking that people like the singer Paul Simon, who had been criticised for going to sing in South Africa, had in fact done more than those who stayed away to undermine the system because he had played and recorded with black musicians and performed to mixed audiences.

I also remembered the Moscow Olympic boycott of 1980. I had been just nine years old and Carl Lewis was one of my heroes. He'd been denied what would have undoubtedly been two or three gold medals because the USA had refused to take part in protest at the Soviet invasion of Afghanistan. As I sat on my bed in Cape Town 23 years later, it was clear US troops were about to invade that same country. And I thought back to my England A tour of Pakistan, where we had been taken to a place near Peshawar on the Afghan border and shown what was basically an arms supermarket. You could buy anything you wanted – Cobra handguns with rounds of ammunition for $50, automatic weapons that could pierce brick walls, AK47 machine guns and a Stinger – a rocket-launcher that would set you back a couple of thousand bucks but came with two shells. Most of the weapons were clearly American and had been supplied to fight the Soviets but were now being sold to fight against US forces. If countries like America could get in such a muddle over what was the right thing to do, what chance had I to make the correct decision?

I phoned John Bird and Frank Dick, who agreed that the decision should not be ours. Graham Gooch, who had been vilified for taking a rebel tour to South Africa, sympathised with our position and was convinced his tour, like Paul Simon's music, had helped to undermine the system from within by coaching black kids. When I asked Keith Fletcher what he thought about the threat by the Sons and Daughters of Zimbabwe, he said, 'Don't let them stop you. We were threatened by Black September, who were a serious crew, and we still played.'

Lorraine said, 'Whatever you decide, I will back you. Just take care.'

I had a secret meeting with Andy Flower in a Cape Town hotel. I wanted to know how he felt as a Zimbabwean. I knew he was a good listener and would give me an honest view. He was opposed to the regime and I was prepared to give a lot of weight to what he thought. I asked him what he was doing.

'I'm going to play,' he said. 'Henry Olonga and I are planning to do something on the day. I can't tell you what it is yet. Look, I perfectly understand that most of the England guys don't want to go. It has to be a personal choice.'

As we found out later, he and Henry wore black arm bands when they played, which I thought was incredibly powerful and brave. If I'd known that was what they had in mind, I think I would have recommended the England team did the same.

Nasser summoned us to a players-only meeting when we would all have a chance to say our piece. I realised one person in our squad was suffering more than most during all this. Duncan Fletcher was a Zimbabwean and was stuck in the middle, so the night before the meeting I went to see him in his room. Even though he didn't pick me very often, I had a lot of respect for Duncan as a coach and as a man. I didn't know what he felt about the situation but, realising that each of the players was going to have to say where he stood, I wanted Duncan to understand that, if my view was different from his, it was not personal. I said to him, 'Duncan, I'm sorry about the position you find yourself in. I just wanted you to know ahead of the meeting that I will be voting to go. Partly it is selfish – cricket is my passion and this is my chance to play in a World Cup – but I also happen to think it is the best way for us to make a protest, to demonstrate support for the oppressed people of Zimbabwe.' He didn't reveal his view either way but he started to well up and so did I.

Nasser had been canvassing opinion before the meeting and called me into the pool room before it was due to start. 'You know you are in a minority of one, don't you?' he said. I thought he was going to tell me to button my lip for the sake of team solidarity, but instead he added, 'What's going on in your head?'

'I believe we should go, Nass. I think we should play in Harare, kick their arses, put two fingers up to Mugabe, then get back here, regroup and get on with trying to win the World Cup. We are cricketers, not politicians.'

'What about the threatening letter, the safety aspect?'

'I don't think there is one.'

'And if there is?'

'Then we'll deal with it.'

At this point all the pressure and tension I'd been feeling welled up in me and I started to cry. Nasser cried too and said, 'I'll say this for you, you're a brave bastard, Irani,' and he walked out of the room.

The players' meeting was one of the most emotional and

bizarre I have ever been involved in as a cricketer. Most were clearly against going, some on moral grounds, some because of the threat, and a few I thought because they were aware of opinion back in England and didn't want to appear to be bad guys. Alec Stewart was torn – he didn't want to be a rebel, but he is a winner in everything he does in life and he desperately wanted the chance to win the World Cup.

When it came to my turn, I said, 'I don't want anyone to take this the wrong way, but I think we should go.' I outlined my views that boycotts made no difference and were just an easy way out for politicians who should be tackling the situation themselves. I repeated that I thought we would do more to undermine Mugabe and give heart to those under his heel by thrashing his team in front of him, and I owned up to the fact that, while I despised the ICC for putting us in this position, I was desperate not to lose the points and damage our chances of winning the World Cup.

One of the lads asked about the threatening letter and I replied, 'I don't believe it.'

'It's real, you've seen it. You can't just ignore it.'

I said, 'I've had lots of threats in my life and they've never come to anything. Even if it is real, it's an attempt at intimidation and bullying and, if I'd let bullies win in my life, I wouldn't be sitting here with you lot.'

There was silence for a moment. Then they all clapped me. Craig White came up and said, 'Great effort, pal. I wish I could stand up and do that.'

'So what do you think?'

'I don't think we should go.'

My powers of persuasion had been so strong that, when it came to the vote, there was only one hand that went up to go! Most of the lads came up and shook my hand and deep down I felt they wanted to be with me from a cricketing point of view but there were too many complications.

I'd had my say: now it was time to shut up, toe the party line and put all my efforts into trying to win the bloody World Cup. It wouldn't be easy – our opening game was supposed to be the one against Zimbabwe on 13 February and the ECB pulled out of it two days before, refusing to travel on safety grounds. After a couple of meetings the ICC awarded the points to Zimbabwe who, having beaten Namibia in their first match, were already eight points ahead of us before we'd bowled a ball.

We had a couple of comfortable wins over the Netherlands and Namibia. I was selected for the second of those matches and was England's leading bowler with three wickets but was left out for the next game against Pakistan. However, another victory meant we still had a chance of being one of the three teams to qualify for the Super Six stage. We really needed to beat India but we came up against Ashish Nehra, the guy I'd caught out at the Oval the summer before, who gained his revenge. And how! Rahul Dravid and Yuvraj Singh helped them to 250 but Nehra never allowed us to threaten in the run chase. I was his final victim in a spell of 6-23 that included Nasser and Stewie in consecutive balls.

Now we had to beat Australia to go through. Ironically, they and Namibia had played in Zimbabwe and there had been no safety problems for either side. The match was to be played on the pitch where I had taken three wickets two weeks before and I knew the conditions were perfect for me. All I had to do was to bowl a good line and length and the batsmen would get themselves out. Nasser agreed when I told him but he and Duncan still decided on Craig White and I had to watch from the balcony.

Nick Knight and Marcus Trescothick gave us a decent start but then Andy Bichel got to work and took seven cheap wickets to restrict us to 205. It seemed that might just be enough on that pitch and things looked good when Andrew Caddick took four early wickets with only 48 on the board. Even after a mini-revival, the best one-day side in the world were struggling on 135-8 when Brett Lee was run out. But Bichel proved as stubborn with the bat as he had been accurate with the ball and provided great back-up for Michael Bevan who was in good nick. With two overs to go, Australia needed 14 to win. Nasser had to make a big call: either bowl Andy Caddick, the experienced campaigner, or Jimmy Anderson, the hot young bowler who was a bit green but had been in superb form throughout the tournament. He went for Jimmy and Bichel hoisted him over mid-wicket for six. Bevan scored the winning runs with two balls left in the game and somehow Australia had escaped.

Nasser came to my room that evening cursing himself for not going with experience but explained he'd been swayed by the thought that Caddick had never done well for him at the death in one-day cricket. I told him not to take it to heart. He'd made the decision he felt was best for the team and he could do no more. It was easy for the armchair experts with the benefit of hindsight to say they would have gone with experience but if I'm honest I might well have made the same decision. These are the kinds of calls you have to make as captain. They don't always work out but you have to be true to your instincts. He didn't need the press to have a go at him: he was beating himself up enough for all of them. His brain was scrambled with the disappointment that we all shared.

Two days later, we watched on TV as Zimbabwe's game

against Pakistan was washed out in a freak Bulawayo monsoon. The two points they picked up were enough to put them above us in the table and we were left to go home and face the music. There was no consoling Nasser and before we left South Africa he announced that he was standing down as ODI captain.

The World Cup had been a massive anti-climax. The whole sorry mess was summed up for me in a news report which read, 'If the ECB and the ICC were batsmen, they would currently be marooned halfway down the wicket shouting, "Yes!" "No!" "Wait!" "Maybe!" in each other's faces, oblivious to the fact that the stumps were already broken at both ends of the pitch. The entire World Cup has been overshadowed by a row that should never have been allowed to develop in the first place.'

As far as I was concerned, we weren't knocked out because of Nasser's decision to bowl Jimmy Anderson, we were eliminated because we hadn't gone to Zimbabwe and I had been brought up to believe that you never give games away. I passionately believed and still believe it was a decision that should never have been left to the players. Tony Blair and his government were loud when it came to saying we shouldn't go, but cowards when it came to making a decision that the ICC would have had to listen to. For all their moralistic talk and the pressure they were willing to put on a group of sportsmen, the politicians still haven't done anything about Mugabe. Even though we didn't play in Harare, the situation in Zimbabwe has got worse and worse and the poor people of that country have been increasingly trodden into the ground. It seems it is easy for politicians to have opinions about what others should do, much harder to take the actions that are in their own hands.

As for cricket's governing bodies, I felt angry that they stubbornly refused to do the right thing and move the game in case they upset TV companies and sponsors. It is typical of the scant respect they have for those who play the game. To them television companies and sponsors are important, while cricketers are just the people who provide the side show and are obviously much less worthy of consideration.

I came back from South Africa knowing my international career was over. There would be no way back this time. I have one souvenir of the trip. Before the game in Zimbabwe was called off, we were given our complimentary tickets for friends and family. I managed to round up some from the other lads as well and asked each member of the squad to sign one. They are now mounted around a team picture with a little brass plate that reads: 'England v Zimbabwe, February 13, 2003. The game that never was.'

CHAPTER 23
POOFS AND PIRATES

While I'd been away on World Cup duty, a series of events for my benefit year at Essex had been put together by my committee under the energetic chairmanship of Anthony Bright and with the indefatigable efforts of the secretary Linda Bennett. They'd pulled out all the stops. In fact, it had started in my absence with a Valentine's Ball in Chelmsford on the day England heard we'd definitely lost the points for refusing to go to Zimbabwe. They'd left me no time to brood on what might have been. My diary was full of events from fly-fishing and golf days as far apart as Bishop's Stortford and Dublin, to a night at Romford dogs and a kick-boxing championship. There was also a series of dinners, including one in the House of Commons and another at the Guildhall in London.

It was while we were discussing arrangements for this that Grant Simmons, as an official at the Guildhall, said to me, 'Ronnie, some Essex fans have written to tell us what you've achieved for the county and the extensive charity work you've done, especially for disadvantaged children. I'd like to put your name forward for the Freedom of the City of London. Would that be OK?'

I said it would be an honour and felt incredibly proud when on 16 April 2004 my name was added to a list of Freemen that includes Winston Churchill, Nelson Mandela and Florence Nightingale. Not bad company. The Freedom, which dates back to 1237 – around the time Alan Brazil was playing for Ipswich – allows me to drive a flock of sheep across London Bridge while drunk and disorderly and wielding a sword. I don't have any sheep but might well walk my Dobermans across one day. As for the alcohol, I might ask if I can pass that privilege on to Al. Not that he is ever disorderly – he's one of those people who becomes mellow with drink, a lover not a fighter, a peacemaker not an aggressor.

Sid Dennis agreed to do a turn at a couple of my dinners and asked if I'd been doing much on the circuit. I told him I'd been too busy with the cricket but the truth was that I'd lost interest after an early date at a rugby club that I'd taken on to help out my mate Jerry Westmore. I'd prepared some new material and, taking Sid's advice, tested it out on Lorraine while she videoed me so I could see where it needed sharpening up. Believe me, it's not easy to make your missus laugh when she's hearing the same routine for the tenth time. But it gave me confidence and I felt pretty good as I made my way to the club. After all, the audience would be intelligent rugby types, not hooligan footballers. Another good lesson in stereotypes for Ronnie.

They were the biggest group of piss heads I've ever encountered in my life. Over the years I've spoken in some of the roughest neighbourhoods in some hard towns, areas where even a 6ft 4in kick boxer thinks twice before venturing out alone. But they have usually turned out to be the places where they pay you before you speak, are always friendly and are among the best gigs. The rugby club was one of the worst.

The meal turned into a food fight. Bread-roll throwing was just the warm-up. Before long all sorts of food was flying about. One guy near where I was sitting picked up a bowl of trifle and just launched it, covering about half-a-dozen people in fruit and custard. I expected a fight to break out but everyone seemed to think it was hilarious. A potato whizzed through the air, bounced off my plate and just missed me. I looked up to find out who had flung it and saw the crust end of a French loaf flying straight towards my head. I caught it like a slip fielder and instinctively threw it straight back where it had come from. It hit the guy who had originally chucked it and he was so drunk it knocked him over. No one took any notice. They just left him crumpled up on the floor.

It was bedlam. I got up to speak and no one was taking the slightest notice. I was halfway through a story when I heard a loud, slurred voice say, 'The pack would like to take wine with the wankers in the backs who fuck up every time we win the ball.' There were loud jeers from one section, 'hear hears' from another, and yet more wine went down the hatch without touching the sides. It was a nightmare. I told myself to ignore them and just remember these tossers had provided the money that was paying me. I cut my speech short, collected my fee and left. I sat in my car and phoned Lorraine. 'Never again,' I vowed.

But Sid had revived the idea in my head and, when I saw guys like Jack Charlton and Gladstone Small stand up and speak at my benefit dinners, I thought I really should give it another go. They seemed to enjoy it and were obviously making good money. I had a word with John Collier, an agent for some of the guys on the circuit, and he thought he could get me work, so I set about putting together some new material. John put me in touch with Ian Richards and Mike Farrell, who are regular after-dinner comedians, and they helped me work up a script based on cricket stories with a few jokes thrown in.

'Keep your gags relevant,' they advised. 'For instance, when you are talking about playing the Aussies you could say, "I landed at Melbourne airport and immigration asked me if I had a criminal record. I replied that I didn't think I still needed one to enter Australia."'

'And remember,' Mike added, 'you've got to keep refreshing the material.'

I took everything on board, worked at polishing my script and I know if I'm stuck for some topical gags I can always rely on Sid or Mike to feed me a few lines to drop in. For instance, when Dwain Chambers tried to salvage his career after his drugs ban by joining Castleford Tigers rugby league club, Mike suggested, 'Say they should change their name to Castleford Cheetahs. Also when Dwain was asked if he wanted tea at half-time, he said, "No, I'll stick to coke."'

Mike also gave me some good tips on dealing with hecklers, although I've been quite lucky and not had too much trouble. You don't want to put them down too badly – after all they are the paying customers – and they could have mates in the room who might turn ugly. Most of the time, I try to win them over like I did the crowd in Australia, or I'll say something like, 'Usually I do this on my own but, if you want to join me and make two of us look like prats instead of one, feel free.' That usually quietens them down.

One night there was a guy sitting just a few yards from me. He was a big fella with a large gold earring and he just wouldn't stop chipping in as I was making my speech. Eventually I decided I had to deal with him so I said, 'Excuse me, pal, but can I help you?' That stopped him talking just long enough for me to add, 'You know, where I come from men who wear earrings are either poofs or pirates and I didn't see any fucking ships in the car park when I arrived.' That brought a big laugh from everybody, including the guy himself, and from then on it all went smoothly.

I really get a buzz out of after-dinner speaking. Just before I stand up to speak, I get the same kind of nerves that I used to feel before I went into bat but that just helps get the adrenaline going. One of my favourite nights was when I was asked to speak in Darren Gough country near Barnsley. They were a great audience and it all went well. The only slight doubt I had was one guy, around 40, solidly built, shaven-headed and I guessed probably an ex-miner or reformed Hell's Angel. He sat with his arms folded all through my speech and never smiled once. At the end when most people were on their feet clapping, he never even twitched. Then he came over, thrust his menu at me and said, 'Sign that, lad.'

As I signed he said, 'Well done tonight. I've been coming here 20 years and you're one of the best I've heard. In fact, you are probably the best.'

I thought he was taking the piss and replied, 'Thank you. I hope you've had a good night. But I have to say from where I was standing it didn't look like it. You never laughed at the jokes and you didn't even applaud at the end. You don't have to be polite – if you didn't enjoy it, say so.'

'Nay, lad. You heard what I said. You're the best I've seen. But it's only a job of work and, when I finish my work at night, no fucker stands up and claps me.'

Anyone who thinks that a player's benefit year involves just arranging some events, turning up and then counting the money should think again. It's hard and quite embarrassing work. You spend a lot of time on the phone trying to persuade people to take a table at a dinner or put a four-ball into a golf day. As Linda pointed out to me, 'They don't want me calling, Ronnie, they want to hear from *you*. I might persuade one in ten to take a table but you are more likely to get seven or eight.' It's not a great job, but, if you want the thing to go well, you've got to work the phone.

One of the ways you make money at these events is to hold an auction of items that people would find hard to get anywhere else, such as a bat signed by the England cricket team or a signed David Beckham shirt. There's quite an art to running an auction and I was recommended to bring in the former Warwickshire captain and TV pundit Dermot Reeve. He agreed to do it and said he could lower his fee if he could bring along a couple of auction items himself, one of which we'd split and one he'd have to boost his fee. I agreed and was impressed when the item he produced for us to share was an album signed by John Lennon. The one for himself was an album signed by Elvis Presley! He ended up almost making more from the auction than I did, but fair dos – he'd only done what I'd agreed to. He'd handled it so well I asked him to come back and run another auction. This time he said he'd bring one item that we would split and again he turned up trumps: a signed photo of Australian cricket legend Don Bradman.

A few days later, Linda told me it was time to get back on the phone and start selling tables at the last few dinners. I started with a call to a good friend – a successful, self-made, local businessman called Mark Anderson. He and his wife Tricia are fantastic, genuine people and had supported a lot of my benefit events, but I sensed a little reluctance when I called him.

'Ronnie,' he said, 'we'll come to the Halloween night but I can't support them all. I've got a budget for this kind of thing and the last dinner cost me quite a lot what with the table and the auction item.'

'Sorry,' I said, 'I'm not sure what you mean. I've seen the list and you didn't buy an auction item last time.'

'Yes I did. I bid for the Bradman photo and didn't get it. Then afterwards Dermot Reeve came up to me and said he'd got another one in the car so I took it and paid him.'

Needless to say, I hadn't seen a penny of that money. In fact, I haven't seen Dermot since then. A couple of years later he resigned from Channel 4 when it came out that he had a £200-a-week cocaine habit. The last I heard he was in New Zealand trying to rebuild his life. I wish him well, but I'd still like to have a word.

Back on the cricket pitch, my young Essex side were struggling to cope with life in Division One again. I'm not sure some of the money men at Chelmsford minded too much, though, because we earned more from getting promotion every other year than we would have done if we'd stayed just above the relegation zone in the top flight – another crazy aspect of the two-division set up. I was struggling a bit with my knee, which kept blowing up, but despite Essex being near the bottom of the table I was reasonably happy that we were heading in the right direction. We had some exceptional young players just beginning to emerge, such as Ravi Bopara, Alastair Cook, Tim Phillips, James Foster, Mark Pettini and Ryan ten Doeschate.

There was a great spirit developing in the dressing room and I knew the young guys trusted me to do what was right for them as well as the club. At one stage some of them were in contract discussions and, knowing there was a bit of leeway in the budget, I advised them to ask for more. It cost the county a few bob, but they could afford it and it helped cement the bond between me and the players. And I genuinely felt they were worth the money they received.

That season saw the start of the phenomenon known as twenty20. It wasn't really new at all – most of us had played something similar at junior level where short matches were staged all the time. But introducing it to the professional arena split the cricket community, with opinions varying from it being the saviour of the game to those who believed it marked the end of civilisation as we knew it. Similar things had been said about one-day cricket when that arrived but I had never agreed with the traditionalists who thought it would wreck Test cricket. On the whole, the best one-day players can step up to Test level but there are a lot of fine five-day players who struggle at the shorter format. And you only have to watch coverage of matches before the introduction of one-day games to see that the standards of batting and fielding have never been higher. These days, you never see a portly old bloke standing applauding a shot from mid-wicket instead of chasing it down to the boundary.

I was all in favour of twenty20 and took to it straight away. I started to open the batting and wished I'd made the change years before. Keith Fletcher always said it was the best place to bat, especially in one-day matches when the fielding restrictions gave you the chance to put on quick runs, and he was dead right. Even though some of the counties had voted against twenty20, I noticed they quickly changed their minds when the crowds started to grow and they could make as much out of one evening game as the whole of a four-day match. Some of the players who had been sniffy about it also began to realise they were missing out. It was the keen, fit, young players who were making an impression and enjoying the adulation of big crowds and some of the older guys needed to get their finger out. Leicestershire were one of the first counties to cotton on to the importance of the game, probably because Grace Road was usually empty and their team were pants at everything else!

There's no doubt in my mind that there is room in the game for all kinds of cricket. There will always be a place for the subtleties of the five-day Test, but equally the Indian Premier League has shown there is a massive demand for the short format. One of the problems that county cricket has – and I'm a big fan of the four-day game – is that the counties are too dependent on the money the ECB hands out from Test matches. While I understand the desire for central contracts for England players to prevent them playing too much cricket, there is no doubt it cuts the attendance at county matches when the big names are not playing.

For the counties to be more independent, they need another big income stream and I think that could come from twenty20. Imagine if every Saturday afternoon during the summer there was a twenty20 league match at grounds round the country, just like football. Better still stage it every Friday night under the lights. I'm sure a good promotions company could soon build up all the old rivalries once again to add a bit of spice: Middlesex v Surrey or Essex, Yorkshire v Lancashire. And put it on terrestrial TV.

I've nothing against the satellite channels – I've worked for both Sky and Setanta – but to me it makes sense for at least some major cricket to be available to people who can't afford a subscription. If the BBC or Channel 4 can't or won't pay the big fees, make up the money through sponsorship and advertising deals. You only have to think back to the Ashes series of 2005 when the whole country got caught up in the cricket. People were captivated because it was on terrestrial TV. I remember driving past a house in the October of that Ashes year and a dad was in the garden bowling to his daughter with his son fielding. Behind the stumps was a football goal but cricket had taken over in their eyes. I was thrilled but also noticed that the house didn't have a satellite dish. Cricket was on a massive upward curve. More than 12 million people watched the final Test of that series and were gagging for more but the authorities let them down. We blew it. Twenty20 on terrestrial TV would give us the chance to win them back and could provide the cash to reinvigorate the county championship, but I wonder if the leaders of our game have the imagination to see the potential or if they will just allow the IPL a free run.

As the season moved towards its completion, it was clear that I needed drastic action on my knee. I was struggling in the field and the only fitness training I could do was cycling, swimming and rowing. Graham Gooch was fantastic. He told me to cut out running in training, realising that I had to protect my knee for on the field. Fortunately, it didn't affect my batting but I knew something had to be done. I'd talked to Jamie Redknapp and asked him about Richard Steadman, a surgeon in Vail, Colorado, who is considered the leading specialist in knee problems. He started his practice dealing with skiing injuries but in recent years has saved the careers of a string of footballers, including Alan Shearer, Craig Bellamy, Ronaldo, Alessandro del Piero and Michael Owen. Jamie couldn't speak highly enough of him so, when I saw David Dandy, the man who had successfully cleaned up my knee a couple of times, I asked him what he thought. He was blunt. 'Ronnie, there's not much more I can do for you. Richard Steadman has a brilliant reputation. I would think he's your best bet.'

It was time to invest in my own future once again. I worked out that with the fares, the accommodation, the operation and the rehab – they start to work on the knee four hours after the operation to break down scar tissue – it was going to cost me around £8,000. But I was as excited as hell about the next few years among what was becoming one of the best dressing-room spirits I'd experienced since the stiffs at Lancashire. I was desperate to be part of it, so anything it cost me would be money well spent. Richard Steadman turned out to be everything people had said about him. He was incredibly positive and encouraging and, when I flew home after the op, I felt sure I'd bought myself some time.

I couldn't wait for the next season to start, especially as my mate Goughie was joining us at Chelmsford.

CHAPTER 24

MIND GAMES TO WIN GAMES

When Darren Gough won *Strictly Come Dancing*, I bought everyone champagne. It was the least I could do – I'd just cleaned up at the bookies at odds of 25–1. Goughie had joined Essex the year before and we were all surprised when he announced he was going to take part in a TV reality show. He admitted he was a bit nervous – 'Bowling in front of a few thousand people in Melbourne is no problem but I'm not sure about this dancing lark,' he said. I told him he'd be fine and said I was so confident that I was going to have a bet on him to win it. The odds then were 15–1 and he told me to save my money because he had no chance. I took his advice but then he got through a couple of rounds and I could see that, while he was not exactly Fred Astaire, he was pretty damn good and, more importantly, the punters loved him. When his odds went out to 25–1, I couldn't resist.

Darren was still unconvinced and used to phone me before the shows so I could gee him up. I said, 'Don't worry about it. These shows are all about personality. Stick your chest out and go for it.'

Just before the final, the BBC wanted a couple of his Essex team-mates to go on a show to air in the lead up to the big night. I think the aim was to show that Goughie's achievement was special by revealing that most cricketers had two left feet when it came to dancing. Graham Napier volunteered and Goughie persuaded me to go along. We had to go to a dance school where world champion Karen Hardy had no time at all to teach us the cha-cha-cha to the Donna Summer tune 'Hot Stuff'. She kept telling me off because I chatted too much and at one stage, when I was supposed to catch her under the arms but instead cupped her breasts by accident (honest!), I thought she was going to give me a slap. Given how little time we had to learn the steps and rehearse, I thought we did an OK job but, when they showed our effort on TV, the general opinion seemed to be that I shouldn't give up the day job.

Goughie was going great guns and, by the time he'd reached the final, he was beginning to feel reasonably confident. I rang him and said, 'So, what do you think of your chances, Daz?'

'I don't know, pal. I'm good, but that Zoe Ball, she's pretty good. And that Colin Jackson is a bit of a dark horse!'

I burst out laughing. I knew Darren didn't have a racist bone in his body and hadn't realised what he'd said. 'I wouldn't say that on the telly if I was you,' I advised.

Lorraine and I went to the final and it was a great night. There was no stopping Goughie. As with everything he does in life, he gave it his all and he thoroughly deserved to win, though I reckon having Lilia Kopylova as his partner didn't harm his chances.

Darren's ability as a dancer was news to me but I'd always known he was a great bowler so I was delighted when he agreed to join us at Essex. I was convinced his never-say-die attitude would rub off on the rest of the team. We had a talented group of youngsters but they still needed plenty of guidance and I knew I could no longer rely on the assistance of Nasser Hussain. Our relationship had fractured for good that summer.

Things had not been good between us for some time. While I understood he wanted to do well for England, I felt he could have given Essex a bit more of his attention. It seemed the only time he was interested in what we were doing was when it suited him – when he needed to get fit again after an injury or get his form back after a lean spell. It felt as though it was more what Essex could do for Nasser than what he could do for his county. It was a situation like that which led to the final breakdown of our friendship.

He'd made it clear from the start that he didn't rate the twenty20 game and didn't want to play in it, so we didn't consider him for selection. Then, when it started to take off with big crowds and he was having a difficult time with England, he suddenly decided he wanted to play. I didn't think that was fair on the lads who had been playing and anyway I didn't believe it was Nass's kind of cricket. There was no time to play yourself in and build an innings, which was his strength, so Graham Gooch decided there was no place for Nass when he picked the team for the next match.

Nass always had problems confronting Goochie. I remember how, in my early days at Essex, we all had to take it in turns to drive the kit van to matches. It wasn't the most popular job in the world and as club captain Graham Gooch was exempt, but the rest of us used to do it, except Nass, who would always find some excuse when it came to his turn.

Eventually, the guy who organised the rota got fed up and raised it with Nass with Goochie in the room.

'Come on, Nass. This is the third time you've ducked out.'

'You can stick your kit van up your arse,' Nass replied.

Goochie overheard and tore him off a strip, saying, if players like Mark Waugh could drive the kit van, so could he. 'Allan Border drove the kit van when he was here and I've driven the kit van. So, if it's good enough for us, it's good enough for you.'

Nasser knew he wasn't anywhere near as good a player as Goochie and certainly nothing like as popular with the Essex fans and I think he felt intimidated by him. So I guess I shouldn't have been surprised that I got the abusive call when he was left out of the twenty20 side. I was driving with Linda Bennett when he came through on the hands-free, so she heard the whole thing.

'All right, Nass?' I asked.

'No, not really.'

'Why, what's up?'

I could tell from his voice he was angry and he soon let me have it. 'You're the fucking matter,' he stormed. 'I've backed you all my career. I've always pushed your cause. If it wasn't for me, you wouldn't have played for England at all. No one else wanted you in the side. I backed you over Stuart Law at Essex and I backed you for the captaincy and this is how you repay me!' After a stream of abuse, he finally asked the question: 'Why am I not in the twenty20 side?'

I was trying hard not to get into a slanging match and said, 'You never made yourself available.'

'Well, I'm available now.'

That completely rubbed me up the wrong way. 'So it suits you to play for Essex now, does it?'

'Yeah, and I want you to do something about it.'

'Ring Goochie. He picks the team.'

'I'm ringing you, you're the captain. I want you to do something about it.'

By this stage, we were both getting heated and talking across each other, so I shut up for another couple of minutes while he sounded off again about how wonderful he'd been to me and that, without him, I'd have been a nobody struggling to make my way. I glanced across at Linda who looked gobsmacked. She was certainly getting a new insight into all for one and one for all.

After a while, I cut in again. 'OK, you've had your say, now let's get a few things straight,' I snapped. 'As far as you backing me to get into the England side, that's a fucking joke. You never backed me. You don't make yourself available for Essex unless it suits you. You pick and choose when you'll play. You're a spoiled brat and always have been. All you care about is yourself. You're a disgrace.'

He tried to cut across me again, but I said, 'No, you listen. You treat people like shit. All you care about is that Nasser is all right. As far as I'm concerned, you can go fuck yourself.'

He hung up. We've seldom spoken since apart from when he interviewed me for Sky, which was uncomfortable for both of us. I bumped into him when I was at the Rosebowl for talkSPORT but when I looked over to him he looked away. I could hear the talkSPORT production lads laughing in my earpiece, saying, 'He really doesn't like you, does he?'

I took the earpiece out and went over to say hello. I knew his dad had recently died and passed on my condolences.

'Maybe we should have a glass of wine one day and catch up,' I said.

'Yeah, that would be good,' he replied.

But I don't think it will happen. It's a shame because I think he does an excellent job on Sky and he was certainly a very fine cricketer and a first-class captain of England. Our characters and approach to the game couldn't be more different but his style of captaincy worked for him and, indeed, I picked up a few things from him that I used when I became skipper. There were several times when dealing with young players that I remembered how Nasser's aggression had brought the best out of people and I did the same.

There had been a few anxious faces around Essex when I suggested we should sign Goughie. We'd played against him the previous season and it was obvious he was struggling with his knees. He could no longer keep going for five days, so his Test career was over and the fact that Yorkshire, where he was a god, were willing to let him go made some people think he was finished completely. He liked the idea of coming to Essex. He and I had always got on, Paul Grayson was his biggest mate and had been best man at his wedding, and Chelmsford was within striking distance of where his sons were living in Milton Keynes. I guess it was something of a gamble but I was convinced that there was nothing wrong with him that Hans Müller-Wohlfahrt and the other specialists in Munich couldn't sort out. With a fit Darren Gough among our young guns, I was convinced we would win trophies. I just needed to persuade Goughie to visit Munich.

'I know your knee is good again now,' I said to him.

'Aye, it's great now,' he smiled.

'But let's take out a bit of insurance. Come and see this guy with me and, if you don't think it helps, that's fine. But there's no harm in trying.'

To be honest, I'd have paid for it myself if necessary. As far as I was concerned, I was getting my Ferrari tuned up for the season and it was worth a few bob to me. But it never came to that. Goughie paid his way to start with and then Alan Lilley said Essex would pay the bills. It was only a few thousand quid, but nevertheless I was delighted he was willing to take my word it was a good investment. Mind you, when he agreed, Alan said, 'Fucking hell, Irani, we'd better win something with all this.'

Goughie was impressed with how good he felt after Hans drained the fluid from his knee and then gave him a Hyalart injection. We also took him to Thomas Mendelssohn to adjust his back and Martin Trautmann for his feet and some new, custom-designed orthotics. As soon as we got the fixture list, we sat down and made appointments with Hans about every three weeks. It was money well spent. Over the next three years, with Darren in the side, we won two major titles and he earned his place back in the England ODI team.

It was important for us to have another experienced bowler in the side because, under advice from Richard Steadman, I was no longer bowling. He had reduced me to tears when he told me I had to pack in. I'd always seen being an all-rounder as a big part of my make-up. I loved to lead from the front in all aspects of the game and in training.

Richard asked, 'Are you telling me you are not good enough to get in the team just on your batting?'

'No. That's not a problem. Batting is my main strength.'

'Well, if you want to still lead your troops from the front, you have to give up bowling. It's the only way to buy you a few more years playing.'

I knew I was going to miss it like hell. I loved the physical endurance and challenge of bowling. There's no better feeling in the world than seeing a ball cut back and knock down the peg of a Brian Lara or Sachin Tendulkar, but I wasn't ready to give up the game I loved. So I accepted that it was time to move on and it paid dividends immediately. My batting went up to a new level and I was chasing people like Andy Flower as the county's leading scorer.

I was also much more settled into the captaincy role and relished the challenge of seeing that an exceptional bunch of players fulfilled their potential. If I'm honest, I was a bit out of my depth when I first took over as captain, but I was determined to learn. I absorbed everything Graham Gooch, Keith Fletcher, John Bird and Frank Dick told me and even went on a man-management course at Ashridge Business School. I also thought back to my days at Lancashire and tried to learn the lessons from how badly they had handled a similar group of hungry young wannabes. I wanted a relaxed atmosphere, where people were comfortable having a beer together and talking about cricket, but I also wanted an honest dressing room, where people could speak their mind without undermining the team spirit. We all had to be able to take criticism as well as praise and I was determined that there would be no bullying of young players.

Some people find it hard to distinguish between bullying and frankness. I've always believed in saying what you think, but only when it is going to do some good. At times, the captain's job is to be brutally honest with someone, but it should always be to help that player improve, not just to put him down. You often hear talk about a coach or captain having to put his arm round someone to get the best out of them and I'm the first to acknowledge there are times when you need to do that. But I discovered something interesting over the years: those who constantly need to be praised are not the players who stand up when the going gets rough on the pitch. They aren't the ones you turn to in a pressure situation or who deliver on the big occasion. To my mind, the ideal player is the one you can push hard and he will respond by giving more.

Ravi Bopara is the ideal example. Keith Fletcher spotted him playing junior cricket and Graham Gooch worked with him from a young age. It was obvious from the start that he had bags of talent and he also had attitude – there were times I would smile because he reminded me of myself when young. I decided to give him his head, knowing that, if he overstepped the mark, I could have a quiet word and he'd acknowledge where he'd gone wrong. And I could push him hard. I could go to Ravi and say, 'That was a joke out there today. You can do a lot better than that,' and I knew he wouldn't sulk or go into his shell. He'd respond by working harder and doing better. If England stick with him, he can go all the way and become a star performer.

When things are going well on the pitch, you hardly need a captain and he certainly doesn't need expensive management courses to get results. It's when the team is struggling that you earn your money. I used to think about the psychology of the game as I drove to the ground, working out how I could turn things round and get the guys firing on all cylinders. I'm not a great believer in relaxing players before a match. To me, if you are not living on the edge, you are taking up too much room. I remember we were about to play against a team we were expected to beat easily and I was determined to make sure the players weren't complacent or taking the game too lightly. I knew we could probably amble to victory but I wanted them to start the game hard and fast and win it as decisively as possible. I went into the dressing room unsmiling and without the usual cheery greetings. I threw my bag in the corner as though I was really pissed off and I stomped around the place a bit. I could see players looking at each other as if to say, 'What's up with Ronnie?'

Just before we went out on the pitch, I gave my team talk: 'Right, you lot, it's a big game. We are streets ahead of this lot but I have to say I'm fucked off with one or two of you at the moment. I'm not going to name names but I need more from you. Your attitude needs to improve. Some of you ponce around as though you've made it but you've won fucking nothing yet. That's what it's about – winning trophies, not posing like tarts. Now get out there and do it today because, if you don't, some of you will have me to answer to.' It was all totally bogus rage but it worked and we slaughtered the opposition with some of the sharpest cricket we'd played.

You have to keep players on their toes. Sometimes when we'd lost, I'd pick on the things we'd done well, and in contrast, when we'd won comfortably, I'd highlight the areas where I'd thought we'd been sloppy. I found that, if you kept your criticism fair and constructive, people would take it on board and, when you'd had a poor game yourself, it was important you held your hand up and admitted it. I liked to let people have their say – and not just those who chip in automatically like that bolshie kid Irani used to, but go round everyone and ask them what they thought. Sometimes the quiet guys were the ones who had thought deepest about the game. And I always made sure I finished on a positive thought that they could take away with them.

I was determined to lead them from the front and wanted them to always be up for the challenge. Sometimes my combative nature saw me in the headlines for the wrong reasons, such as when I pulled a fast one over Shane Warne and he responded with typical Aussie aggression.

Without doubt, the best two spinners in my time in cricket were Shane and Muttiah Muralitharan. Murali is a really nice bloke but I've always thought his action bends the rules far more than any of the dubious practices associated with reverse swing. The first time I faced him, I didn't have a clue where the ball was going to bounce. There was so much fizz on it and I couldn't read it out of his hand. I was completely bamboozled. Gradually, I worked out the angles and learned to play him. It was easiest with the white ball where the seam was clearer – if the seam was straight, it was the orthodox delivery; if it was scrambled, it was going the other way.

He is an outstanding talent and it's a shame that he will always have a question mark against his action. I wonder if there is not a case for changing the law to accommodate players like him. After all, he is never going to break a batsman's arm, so there is no real danger as there would be with a quick bowler who bent his arm.

There was never any question about Warney's action. It was perfect. He hardly ever bowled a bad ball and had an incredible variation all apparently from an identical delivery. His 'flipper' could be devastating. I first heard about him when he was a youngster playing for Accrington in the Lancashire League. The stories coming back were that he was a fun-loving Aussie who enjoyed chips and beer, and bowled a few leggies. They were smacking him around for fun but, before you knew it, he was knocking Mike Gatting over in a Test at Old Trafford and a legend was being born. I doubt we will ever see anyone else of his class in my lifetime.

There was always a bit of needle in matches between Hampshire and Essex and, when Shane arrived as their captain, he was certainly ready to hype things up. We turned up to play them at the Rose Bowl in one of his first games in charge. Whenever you play down there, you want to bat first because the pitch is going to get worse as the days go by. But this was a damp morning and I admit to a few doubts and thought about letting the bowlers have a go at them but then decided against it. As Shane and I went out to the wicket to toss up, I sensed he too was unsure and thought I might be able to work it to my advantage.

He's a big poker fan so I wondered if he was testing me when he said, 'Not the normal Rose Bowl wicket.'

'Yeah, you're right. You normally know what you're going to do here but I have to admit I'm not so sure today. I think I've gone the other way looking at that.'

Now I was certain he was wavering and, to ram home my advantage, I squatted down and rubbed my hand over the grass on the wicket. 'Bloody hell,' I said. 'That is wet.'

The coin went up and I lost the toss. 'Your call, mate,' I said. 'I don't think that's a bad toss to lose.'

'Yeah. You have a bat.'

If I'd been a better actor, I would have winced. As it was, it took an Oscar-worthy performance for me to suppress a huge grin. I suppose there was a possibility that we could have been knocked over for 80 but we saw off the early overs and were on the way to making 416, inflicting Hampshire's heaviest defeat for 108 years.

By the time I went in to bat, Shane was not a happy man. He started to sledge me before I'd even reached the crease. 'Here he is, Mr Essex. Strange how nobody likes him at the club. None of them want him there.' He couldn't possibly have been talking to Stuart Law, could he? He continued to have a go throughout my innings with some pretty personal stuff. Even when I was at the non-striker's end, he was rabbiting away and the umpire just stood there and said nothing. His team-mates took their lead from him, and they started to join in. I was determined not to react or to let it affect me, although I was boiling inside.

I almost snapped when someone, not Warne, made a filthy comment about my mother, but I wasn't going to let them see they were getting to me. My jaw ached from clenching my teeth in concentration. I was just as angry at the umpires as I was at Shane and the Hampshire players – the pair of them were gutless and never said a word.

I was still at the wicket when play stopped for the day. I thought, Right, now it's my turn. I asked my batting partner, Paul Grayson, to take my helmet and bat and went over to Warne and said, 'Right, what's your fucking problem?'

He looked startled and muttered, 'Not here, mate. Not on the pitch.' And he started to walk off.

I shouted after him, 'Hey, where do you think you're going? I'm talking to you. I want to know what your fucking problem is. You've been slaughtering me big time. If you're such a big man, let's have it out here, face to face.'

The other Hampshire players started to walk towards me. I yelled across, 'You lot can fuck off. You've all been standing there while he's been abusing me and done nothing. All you do is suck his cock. I'll take you lot as well if you want.'

Warne had slunk off by now and, as I left the pitch, I got some stick from the Hampshire fans. I turned on one guy and said, 'How would you like it if your mother was called a whore?'

The next morning, Shane and I were summoned to the umpires' room and they said, 'We have to do something about this.'

Shane looked innocent and said, 'About what, mate? What's the problem?'

'It got too heated out there. We are going to have to put a report in. We don't want to see any repetition.'

I said, 'Hang on a minute. It's not just me and Shane involved. He was giving me stick for ages and you two blokes did nothing about it. No wonder it got heated.'

I was obviously getting nowhere and decided to shut up and take whatever consequences arose. Shane stuck out his hand and said, 'Let's move on.' I took his hand but he wasn't looking me in the eye, so I hung on. Eventually, he looked up and gave me a nod, and we went out and finished off stuffing them in the match.

Somehow, a journalist heard or was told what I'd said to the fans and there was a headline in the *Daily Mail*: 'Irani: Warne called my mum a whore'. Shane rang me and I said, 'I know you didn't say that. Don't worry – I'll put the record straight,' which I did and I also put it in writing to him. He's a hell of a competitor. On that occasion, I felt he'd gone much too far, maybe because he felt I conned him over the wicket. But, whatever his reason, it could have all been nipped in the bud by the umpires and need never have got as ugly as it did.

The next few years were among the most enjoyable of my career. With no bowling to do, I had more time to spend on my batting, while the energy and ambition of the young players around me gave me renewed enthusiasm for the game. It wasn't always easy. We had to ask Paul Grayson, a good mate for many years, to take up a new, non-playing role and we let Darren Robinson go, to make room for the youngsters. But part of the job of a captain is to do what is best for the club in the long term, even when that is painful.

As well as Goughie and Andy Flower, we were boosted by

the arrival of Danish Kaneria, a fine leg-spin bowler who won us a lot of matches with really tight bowling in the middle of an innings. I've always said that a captain is only as good as his bowlers and, thanks to these guys, I was now a much better captain. In 2005, we won the Totesport National League one-day trophy, a competition described by Keith Fletcher as probably the hardest to win. We were unstoppable, losing only one match in 16 and clinching the title with three games to go. The following year, we retained it, although it was a much tighter margin.

I was starting to think about just how far this team could go. Essex hadn't won a county championship since 1992 and I knew that would mean a lot to the members. But my knee was playing up again and I needed to go back to see Richard Steadman in Colorado. What he said changed my life.

CHAPTER 25

I'LL BE FRANC, IT'S FRIGHTENING

Vail, Colorado is stunning. A relatively recent town, it nestles high in the Rockies among huge mountains and ski slopes. It only has a population of around 5,000 people but each year around three-quarters of a million arrive to enjoy the spectacular scenery, the fresh air and the local sport. I was one of those limping before I got near the ski slopes!

I'd hoped Richard Steadman would be able to fix me up and send me back fighting fit to finish the 2007 season. I firmly believed I was captaining a side that could go places and I was in some of the best form of my life. I'd averaged in the high 50s for each of the three previous seasons and I'd already scored 465 runs in the first four county championship matches, including a career-best 218 against Glamorgan in front of the fans at Chelmsford. That was one of the most enjoyable knocks of my life – I went past my previous best 207 with an on drive for six off Alex Wharf, and Ryan ten Doeschate and I were only four short of a record sixth-wicket stand for Essex when he pulled a long hop into the hands of Robert Croft in trying to reach his 150.

All through my career, I'd tried to play every ball as though it was my last, but somehow I never thought it would be. But I had aggravated my knee against Leicestershire and, when he examined it, Richard pulled no punches. 'Ronnie,' he said, 'it is time to stop. I could patch you up and you could play on perhaps another season, but then you would be facing a complete knee replacement in your forties and that is not to be recommended. You have the rest of your life to look forward to with your family. You are going to want to do things and go places with Simone and Maria but there's a danger that you won't be able to, certainly not pain-free. It's your decision, but I think you should stop.'

It took a while to sink in and when it did, I was gutted. However, when I cleared the emotion away, it was a no-brainer. If the best specialist in the world couldn't help me, then no one could. I'd always said that cricket was just the stepping stone to the rest of my life and now it was time to accept that the first stage was over. I'd had 19 years being paid to play the game I loved. I'd given it my all but, as much as I knew I would miss it, I had to let my head rule my heart.

I went back to Essex and asked for a meeting with the committee. Some of the people I admired most were in the room. It was particularly poignant that Graham Gooch and Graham Saville, who had played such a big part in my career, were there as I told my county the news. They had offered me a lucrative new two-year deal just before I went to Vail and a couple of old pros suggested I should sign it quickly but that didn't seem right. These people had always been straight with me. I'd never even had to negotiate a new contract: each new one they offered me was for at least the going rate, sometimes more. My final deal had been for three years with an increase built in each year. There were times when I could have gone elsewhere and earned another ten or twenty grand, but that wouldn't have been sufficient compensation for leaving a club and fans that I enjoyed working for. I remember reading Roy Keane's book where he said he took a lower wage than other clubs were offering to join Manchester United because it felt right. That's how I felt about Essex.

I told the committee that Richard had told me I might be able to play on and they said they would back any decision I took. I found it hard to say the words, but finally I said, 'You've always been fantastic to me. It wouldn't seem right spending half the time in the physio's room and taking 100 per cent of the money. I think my time is up.'

We made the announcement and a few nights later I said my farewell to the fans who meant so much to me, walking around the packed Chelmsford ground with Simone and Maria.

Any player will tell you that when you retire you quickly forget about the pain and the frustrations and just miss the day-to-day contact of the dressing room and the rush you get when the crowd reacts to what you do on the pitch. I've never taken drugs because my life has always supplied natural highs, but I imagine going cold turkey must be similar to the way I felt for some time after I quit playing. There was an enormous hole. There was too much time. There was no buzz.

I don't like using the word depression – it's bandied about too much by people who are just feeling low – but I think I came close to it in the weeks following my retirement. I can certainly understand why some ex-sports stars turn to drugs or booze. I was surrounded by memories of a career I'd relished, including trophies I'd picked up as a kid. I hired a skip and shoved them all in it, and have to admit I smiled when someone rang me to say they'd bought one of my Under-12 football cups at a car-boot sale. At least my disappointment had given somebody some pleasure.

I needed to get on with the rest of my life and I certainly found plenty to occupy me when Nick Bones, who had built my house, invited me to join him at a property auction at Dunmow in Essex. We'd worked together on two or three developments and he said this one might be quite interesting. 'There's a bit of land I like the look of but I think it might go for a lot more than I want to spend,' he said. 'It's got a house on it already and planning permission for another. If you like, we can go halves on it.' Nick had set his limit at £300,000 and, as it didn't look as though that would be anywhere near enough, I didn't bother to tell Lorraine the details of where we were going and why.

It was a bleak November day with the rain almost horizontal on a cold wind. The auction house was half-empty and the auctioneer was struggling to get business going. When he reached the lot we were interested in, he tried to start it at £300,000 but didn't pick up a bid until he dropped down a hundred grand. He was working his socks off and gradually moved it up to £235,000 when I heard Nick call out, 'Two hundred and forty!'

Oh shit, I thought, I've just spent a 120 grand. What am I going to tell Lorraine? Fortunately, another couple of bids came in and I sighed with relief.

'Two hundred and sixty.' It was Nick again!

I waited for a counter-bid but after a brief pause I heard the auctioneer say, 'I'm selling at 260. Are we all done? Going once, going twice... Are we all done at 260? Sold for £260,000!'

Nick punched the air. I stood there with a silly grin on my face, trying to frame the words that would tell Lorraine how clever I had been to spend £130,000 of our savings on a field in Dunmow. Surely I could convince her it was a good investment? I was less confident when, as I handed over a cheque for the deposit, a guy came up to us and said, 'I own the land next to the piece you've just bought – how would you like to buy that?' Before I could say a word, Nick said, 'Yes, please.' We were then offered the land on the other side with planning permission for a bungalow. By now, it felt as though I was dealing with Monopoly money. I just hoped the next card I picked up didn't say: 'Go direct to jail. Do not pass Go and do not collect £200.'

If I have any good advice for men out there, it is choose a wife who is unflappable in a crisis and who says 'Que sera sera' when faced with her husband stretching their bank balance to its limit. It's not that Lorraine is blindly willing to put up with anything I do, it's just that she believes there are a lot more important things in life than money, although, as this saga stretched its wayward course and we came close to losing our home, I must admit there were times she questioned my financial acumen. But, hey, I'd done such a good job with the dot.com investment of our mortgage money, I was sure I was on a roll!

I needed to raise more cash and it was suggested I took out a foreign currency loan against the value of my house. The theory is simple: you borrow money in a currency with low interest rates, and convert it to a currency with higher deposit rates. That would cover the interest payments and make me a handsome profit! For example, you borrow Swiss francs and switch to the pound. At the time of borrowing, Swiss francs were costing two per cent per annum and after conversion were receiving interest at five per cent, a gain of three per cent. This works if the exchange rate between the two currencies remains stable or in your favour, as you need to buy Swiss francs to pay the interest payments. With the pound going great guns and a new job at talkSPORT, I was flying. Or I would have been if it hadn't been for a little local difficulty with an accountant which ended up costing me thousands of pounds.

Thankfully, I had a superb solicitor who I'd met through John Bird. It is fair to say that Michael Wright doesn't fit the usual image of a solicitor. He starts work at 2.30am because the phones won't be ringing, and he sits there with R&B blasting out with heavy bass as he solves his clients' problems. Several times I went round for a meeting at 5.30am before going on to play in a match. I trusted him completely and, even though it cost me money, he eventually freed me from the clutches of that London accountant.

I was still concerned about my situation with the foreign loans which were no longer looking such a good idea as the pound started to weaken. I couldn't sleep at night, worrying about what I should do. I just didn't know enough to sort it out myself. I phoned Alison Monk, who had tried to help me with earlier share problems, and said, 'I need to talk to someone who is red hot.'

'I've got just the man,' she said. 'Richard Nixon.'

Even in the state I was in that made me laugh. But once again she turned out to be spot on. I met him in Barclays' magnificent offices in Canary Wharf and was immediately impressed by him. He was young and dynamic, a no-bullshit guy. Just like Hans Müller-Wohlfahrt, he handled the matters he was good at and passed me on to others to sort out areas he didn't specialise in. Between Richard,

David Pearce (a specialist in foreign currency deals) and Keith Carrington (who became my new bank manager), they got to grips with the whole of my financial situation. It wasn't great. David warned me that the way the market was going I was in danger of being £200,000 out on my loan and I had some hard decisions to make. I was summoned to a meeting in the West End and told to bring all my documents with me. I did more than that. I took along Linda Bennett (because by this time she was running my office and had all the figures at her fingertips), my new accountant Meher Tengra and Lorraine, because it was her future too.

We were introduced to Paul Shrimpton, a senior executive at Barclays, who appeared to be the person who would have the final say on whether or not the bank would back the scheme to get me out of the mire. He was very straightforward and spelled out all the options. He said that things had improved slightly – I was only down £80,000 now – but that the market was still volatile. I could leave the money where it was and hope it would continue to improve or I could switch to sterling and they would give me a loan to make up the difference. We looked at the figures and I realised that if we switched now I could still afford the payments, but if we left it and things got worse we might lose our home. It was time to take it on the chin. We switched back into sterling.

It was a chastened group that went over the road to a restaurant for coffee. There were a few tears, partly of relief but also at the realisation at how close we had come to possible ruin. Once again I had learned some valuable, if expensive lessons. Firstly, if a scheme seems too good to be true, it probably is. Secondly, the best advice might cost more but if you pay peanuts you get monkeys. These people had sorted out my position and I was able to look to the future with some optimism.

It was good to shed all that anxiety over money. I needed to concentrate on my new radio career.

CHAPTER 26
WHAT'S IT ALL ABOUT, ALFI?

I grew up in a household where racing was a regular part of the TV diet and the sport had always excited ne. I had favourite horses like Oh So Sharp and Commanche Run but probably top of the list was Dancing Brave. I can still clearly recall the thrill when watching the 1986 Arc and hearing the commentator say, 'And here comes Dancing Brave!' It was just awesome watching Pat Eddery bring him on a devastating late run to triumph by over a length in record time, leaving the rest of the field trailing, including Shahrastani who had beaten him in the Derby.

So you can imagine how much I enjoy the fact that on *Sports Breakfast* I regularly get to talk to top trainers and Channel 4's legendary race presenter Derek Thompson, one of my heroes. It has also allowed me to get to some of the great race meetings like Cheltenham and Ascot, though our trip to Ascot became a bit hairy when Lorraine flushed the car keys down the loo and we had to race for a train! Mind you, just as working with Al makes you keep an eye on your alcohol intake, I have to make sure I don't get led astray in my regular chats to Thommo and Simon Clare and Dave Stevens of Coral, and turn an occasional flutter into a betting habit.

Joining talkSPORT has allowed me to indulge my passion in a wide number of sports and also to get to grips with the medium. I love speech radio. I believe it has an enormous future simply because it connects directly with listeners wherever they are and it gives them the chance to be heard. I wanted to be part of it so, when I landed the job as Alan Brazil's sidekick, I decided that once again I needed to invest in my own future. I worked with Liam Fisher and Mark Smith at talkSPORT on the basic techniques and then signed up with a company called Alfi Media, run by two former 5 live staffers who offered media training. Alison Rusted had produced a whole string of big shows, including 5 live's Olympic and rugby World Cup coverage, and royal weddings and funerals. Fiona Cotterill had worked on things as varied as parliamentary reporting and the Simon Mayo show. They'd worked with other ex-pros like Gary Lineker and Ally McCoist and I couldn't have asked for better coaches.

They really knew what they were talking about and taught me some of the tricks of the trade, helping me to come across as more relaxed and natural, while still handling the technical stuff behind the scenes. It was bloody hard work and at times a bit bruising to the ego. Several times a week, I would go straight from the talkSPORT studio to see them and they would analyse that morning's broadcast and suggest ways I could improve. They didn't pull any punches but I knew that, if I wanted to get better, I had to take it on the chin and put what they told me into practice. They worked on my interview technique and jumped on one of my early bad habits – cutting across Al when he was in full flow. 'Less is more,' Ali said. 'When he's on a roll like that, just sit back and let him go, otherwise you get car-crash radio.'

Thanks to their help and the support of the *Sports Breakfast* team, I gradually became more confident and relaxed doing the show. I like to get in early, around a quarter to five, and go through all the papers to see what's happening. I'm still surprised at the incredible energy levels there are in the studio at that time of the morning, especially as there's not so much as a slice of toast to keep us going! We have a great team – young, bright and ambitious and most of all dedicated to doing the best show they can. Warren Haughton and Gilo Carruthers line up some of the interviews and send me an email so I have a chance to think about the things I want to talk about. There's always a million ideas flying about from people like Josh Milligan, Dave Richards, Owen Jones, Kate Wood and Richard Boullemier, who do so much of the work behind the scenes. Faye Carruthers delivers precise news, 'The Moose' Ian Abrahams is a classic sports enthusiast who loves arguing and getting pelted, and Eddie Salim (DJ Ed) is a legend. They are a lively bunch and take their cue from Liam Fisher and the boss Moz Dee. Scott Taunton is the managing director who combines being an astute businessman with his enthusiasm for the medium. His only weakness is an over-optimistic view of how good the Australian cricket team is.

Alan Brazil and I hit it off straight away and the chemistry started to come across in the programmes. We talk to each other as though we were back in a dressing room, teasing and joking but also talking frankly about the issues. The listeners want a laugh and some banter at that time of the morning, but they also tune in to hear the perspective of a couple of blokes who know what it's like to be in the arena and who know some of the people involved. I was always close to the fans as a player and quickly realised that it is a mistake to try to bullshit them. They know when someone isn't putting in the effort or a team isn't performing to its potential, and it's no good trying to kid them otherwise. I love taking the phone calls and chatting to listeners and quickly learned that there are plenty of times when the only thing you can say is: 'I'm not sure I agree but you've made a good point.'

Different viewpoints are what makes speech radio interesting but of course you get the odd numpty who just wants to be abusive, such as the guy who phoned in to complain when I criticised Chelsea players' behaviour after they were knocked out of the Champions League by Barcelona.

'Hey, Irani. I'm sick of you criticising Chelsea.'

'OK, pal. But my name is Ronnie.'

'Look, Irani...' and he launched into a tirade.

I tried to persuade him to have a proper discussion but he wouldn't have it, so I faded him down and said, 'Now, the listeners can't hear you. For the last time, my name is Ronnie. Are we going to discuss this like grown men who can disagree but be polite?' I faded him back up.

'Irani, you've just...' The producer cut him off and we moved on.

The part of the job I like best is interviewing the guests. I love the fact that I can talk to some of the biggest names in sport, some of the stars I've admired for years. We are very fortunate because people who are usually wary of the media know we are as passionate about sport as they are and that we see our role as informing and entertaining, not trying to stuff them. Our job is to try to cover the questions the listeners would ask, but also to use our knowledge of being the guy facing the fast bowler or taking the penalty to draw out some insights. There are times when you have to ask a hard question – throw in a bit of reverse swing rather than a gentle full toss – but Ali and Fiona taught me there are ways of doing that which are fair and give the other person the opportunity to make his or her case.

Just as a batsman expects the odd bouncer, most interviewees are ready with their answer to the tough questions. Many of them have also been to companies like Alfi to learn how to handle such situations. I presume former England manager Steve McClaren had received such media training because he was more like a politician than a football manager after the 'wally with the brolly' international. No matter what I asked him, Steve answered a question he would have preferred to have been asked. I tried to put the question another way and he just smiled and talked about something else. In the end, I had to give up and move on or I'd have broken Jeremy Paxman's record of asking Michael Howard the same question 12 times.

In stark contrast to that was the interview with Dwain Chambers, who came into the studio to plug his book. I have no time for people who use drugs to cheat at sport, so I was expecting to dislike him. But he came across as a really nice guy, not at all cocky and genuinely contrite. He didn't try to blame anyone else or moan about the fact that he'd been caught when others had got away with it. He put his hands up, admitted he'd made mistakes and explained why he'd made them, while agreeing that reasons were not excuses. There was still a bit of an edge to the interview – he had disgraced himself but to my mind his biggest failing was that he had also robbed his three relay team-mates of a medal – but I ended up respecting him. I suppose, if you believe that everyone around you is cheating with drugs, that might justify your joining them. I hate that side to athletics.

What with talkSPORT and regular after-dinner speaking, I was keeping busy. I was also pleased I'd followed another piece of good advice from John Bird, who said, 'If you're getting up at 3.30 in the morning and going to dinners all over the country that finish late at night, you are going to need a driver. Otherwise you'll fall asleep at the wheel and kill yourself.'

He was right. I now have the pleasure of the company of Dave Callan and, judging by the number of times I fall asleep in the car, John's assessment was spot on. I wouldn't be able to function without a driver.

I usually get home from talkSPORT about midday, so for the first time in the girls' lives I'm around to pick them up from school and spend some time with them, which is a massive bonus. I thought that I would probably sleep in the afternoon, but I find it almost impossible and much of my time is spent working on products for my company. Many ex-sportsmen have their own businesses, most of them rather glamorous. Former Southampton striker Mick Channon is a racehorse trainer, Imran Khan became a politician, Eric Cantona a film star. I decided to go into insoles.

I'd been wearing insoles as shock absorbers in my cricket boots since I was 14 years old and knew the benefits. My view on how essential they are grew even stronger when I discovered podiatry in New Zealand, and then later in Germany Martin Trautmann added years to my career with the customised insoles he created for me. Martin explained to me that most injuries start from the ground up and his insoles would not only make my feet more comfortable, but they would also take a lot of pressure off my knees. I became fascinated by the subject, and the more I went into it, the more I thought we should join forces in some kind of business. I wondered if it was possible to produce a top-quality insole that would benefit a lot of people without the high cost of one made to a specific prescription. To my delight, Martin said it was what he had always dreamed of doing, but didn't have sufficient time or contacts.

I got in touch with Aimee and Damian Donzis, two friends of mine in the States, who I knew were interested in the subject and had contacts with manufacturers in China. They sent over a sample of a new material called Poron that has great shock absorbency and Martin incorporated it into his design. We all felt we were on to a potential winner but it took more than three years to get the insole exactly how we wanted it. It was an expensive process – by now Aimee and Damian were working full-time in the company – but we refused to take shortcuts and went for quality. We made up some samples and gave them to Darren Gough, Alex Tudor and Jamie Redknapp to try out. All three were very positive and I was sure we had a product that had enormous potential. While insoles may not be glamorous, there is a huge market for them – one company in America sells more than a million a year – and their use is becoming more and more recognised by the medical profession as a way to deal with ailments from dodgy knees and hip problems to bad backs.

We took out the necessary patents and I decided it was time to try to test the market here. We appointed a couple of reps in the UK and Nic White got us into key outlets in the south like Harrods and chemists John Bell & Croyden, while Adam Hill, our guy in the north of England, arranged for me to visit DLT in Huddersfield, one of the top wholesalers serving podiatrists across the country.

As Dave drove me up the M1 towards Huddersfield, I was feeling a bit nervous. There was a lot riding on this meeting: many hours of work and no small sums of cash had gone into the development. I couldn't afford to screw it up. I was a bit concerned because I'm just an ex-cricketer with an enthusiasm for podiatry while the people I was about to talk to are real experts. I told myself that in the background I had the undoubted knowledge of Martin Trautmann so, if I didn't know the answers to their questions, I could always find out and get back to them. Nevertheless, I would have been happier facing the most hostile bowler in the world than walking into that office to meet Darren Sandy, senior executive and great-grandson of the founder.

I showed him the insole and he was clearly impressed. He called his partners in to take a look.

'What's your involvement?' he asked. 'Are you just endorsing them?'

'No. I'm a partner in the company. For the last three years I've been investing my own money to get them to this stage. I really believe in these things and how they can help people from all walks of life.'

The meeting had been due to last an hour but it stretched on as they enthusiastically discussed the potential of our orthotic. I finally got away just after 7pm but by the time I got home I was too excited to snatch even a couple of hours' sleep and made my way to the studio knackered but happy. It is still early days but one thing is certain: if the company doesn't work, it won't be for the want of trying.

Meanwhile, I've just signed a new deal with talkSPORT and I'm really excited about the next few years. I feel comfortable behind the mike these days and now, just as I did with cricket, I want to keep working at it and get as good as

I possibly can. I'm very fortunate to be working alongside Al, who continues to be generous with his help and has become a true friend. Mind you, he has his shortcomings, one of which is a cavalier approach to organisation, as I discovered soon after I joined the *Sports Breakfast* team.

The trip to see Ricky Hatton fight Floyd Mayweather in Las Vegas started with one of those taxi-driver moments that prevent people in the public eye from becoming big-time charlies. I had hailed a cab outside the office and said, 'Heathrow, please.'

I could see the cabbie looking quizzically at me in his mirror as though he recognised the face but couldn't put a name to it. I smiled back at him. He kept looking and I started to reach into my briefcase for one of the photos I carry around in case I bump into an Essex fan who wants an autograph.

'OK, mate,' he said, 'give us a clue.'

'Cricket, Essex, England, talkSPORT, Alan Brazil's *Sports Breakfast* show...'

'No, mate. Which bleedin' terminal?'

This wasn't an official talkSPORT trip. Alan had come up with the idea of spending a couple of nights in Vegas to take in what promised to be one of the fights of the year, plus a few bottles of bubbly and maybe chance our arms on the roulette wheel. We were paying our own way. 'Don't worry,' he said, 'my mate Ticket Ted from Teddington will take care of everything.'

I was looking forward to a fun weekend but some of the gloss was rubbed off when we arrived in Vegas to find our luggage hadn't joined the same connecting flight at Los Angeles as we had.

As we stood around the carousel waiting to see if the bags

would turn up, some of Ricky's Manchester City fans recognised me. I think it is fair to say they had been sampling the drinks trolley since taking off in England and they weren't pleased to see me. Their main complaint was that I was a Man U fan and had moved from Lancashire to Essex. Perhaps it was the alcohol but they certainly seemed to have trouble remembering my name. 'Fucking Judas' was among the more polite alternatives they came up with. The abuse grew even louder and more extreme when they spotted Alan, who had had the temerity to play for Manchester United.

After a tiring day, a long flight, the crossing of several time zones, lost luggage and intimidating abuse from strangers, Alan said, 'Fuck it, I'm not going to the fight. We'll only get a load more stick and maybe worse. By then they will be completely legless and probably throwing things.'

So we ended up playing the tables instead. I'm not a big gambler but I like a punt now and again and that night won around $1,500. We had an excellent meal, a glass or two of wine and a jolly evening. I finally watched Mayweather knock out Ricky on TV when I got home.

Getting home sounds simple enough but I realised it might not be so straightforward when I asked Al what time our flight left Vegas the next day. He said, 'Dunno. Don't worry, Ted's taken care of it all,' and popped the cork off another bottle of champagne. I eventually made my way over to Ted, who said, 'Nothing to do with me. You should have all your tickets and details.' I had nothing.

Alan was completely unconcerned and had decided he was enjoying himself so much that he was going to stay over another night anyway. But, while talkSPORT had learned to live with him occasionally going AWOL, I was a new boy and didn't want to blot my copybook this early in my career.

When I rang the airport to check, we had already missed our flight to LA and therefore our connection to London. I spent a couple of hours on the phone desperately trying to find a flight that would get me back in time to go to work and eventually managed to arrange a seat that got me in by the skin of my teeth at the cost of £850 on my credit-card bill.

Working alongside Al – and occasionally playing, although my stamina is not as good as his! – is never dull and has been so important to me. He knew what I was going through when I finished playing cricket and has shown me how to channel all my energies into new challenges rather than just wishing I was still out in the middle. He also geed me up when I faced criticism early on. I knew I was no Terry Wogan but I was working hard to improve and some of the comments hurt. Al just said, 'Ignore them. You're doing fine. Some people just like to have a pop. They'll pick on someone else soon.' As usual, he was right.

I'm often asked if I will ever go back into cricket as a coach. With everything else I have on at the moment, it seems unlikely, certainly in the immediate future. But I did enjoy being captain of Essex and you can never say never. I like to be part of a team and if I was to take charge of a club I'd want to surround myself with good specialist coaches and medical staff. I was always struck that, while the England set-up had loads of PR people, officials and even IT staff, they only had one batting and one bowling coach. That seemed crazy to me. What's more important – running round after the press or making sure your players are in peak mental and physical condition? I also believed that too often the coaching staff behaved like school teachers handing down their wisdom from on high, rather than working with the players in a way that they can relate to. I doubt that any club would make the investment in staff that I would want to do the job the way it should be done. But it's a shame because, with the talent we have in this country, we should never be trailing behind Australia, India and South Africa.

I had a fantastic time playing cricket, met some extraordinary people, travelled the world and will always look back on those days with huge satisfaction and happiness. Would I have liked to play more for England? Of course, but I have no complaints and my career at Essex more than made up for any disappointment on the international front.

I never believe people who say they have no regrets when they look back over their life. I am sorry that I'm no longer close to some of the great friends I had when I was young. I know a few of them think I deserted them when I became a pro but it really wasn't like that. It's all down to circumstances and choices that you have to make. If I was going to make it as a cricketer, I couldn't spend nights out on the lash. I had to be more focused and give up some of the things I'd enjoyed before and, in doing that, inevitably you grow apart from people. Moving to Essex changed things a lot as well. It wasn't just me who moved on: when I went back it was great catching up on old times with mates, but we didn't have any new times to share. It even happened within the game. John Crawley and I were like brothers at one stage but our careers went off in different directions and we drifted apart. It's very sad but I guess it's inevitable.

The other side of the coin is that some people don't want to stay in touch with you. I allowed myself a wry smile when my pal Dexter Fitton phoned me to tell me he'd received a letter from Lancashire County Cricket Club inviting him to a reunion. 'You're on the list, Ronnie,' he said, 'as one of the people they've been unable to contact!' They couldn't have tried very hard.

I still see the lads at Essex. I'm on the cricket committee and follow their fortunes and I'm thrilled by the success Ravi Bopara is having with England, but clearly it's not the same as being in the dressing room every day. However, I believe passionately in the advice Frank Dick once gave me: 'Achievement is a journey without an ending and the hardest part of planning is how to arrive at one destination and look forward to the next.'

My aim now is to put the same enthusiasm and energy into my life as a broadcaster and any other opportunities that come my way as I did in my cricket. Every single day I try to look forward, with no boundaries.